RECIPES FROM THE CHÂTEAUX

OF THE

Loire

Gilles du Pontavice
Bleuzen du Pontavice

Collection edited by
BLEUZEN DU PONTAVICE

Photographs
CLAUDE HERLÉDAN

Translation by
ANGELA MOYON

EDITIONS OUEST-FRANCE
13, rue du Breil, Rennes

The châteaux in the Loire Valley have a long history but the best-known houses along the river banks are linked to the presence of the Court during the reign of the Valois kings, a dynasty founded in 1328 by Philip VI. It came to an end in 1589 with the death of Henry III. It was in an effort to protect himself against the civil war raging in Paris in 1418 that the son of Charles VI the Mad, the Duc de Touraine et de Berry, heir to the throne, sought refuge in the residence of his mother, Yolande of Aragon. He was a frequent visitor to her château in Melun-sur-Yèvre and it was here, in later years, that Joan of Arc was knighted.

On the death of Charles VI in 1422, his son, Charles VII, succeeded him but his claim to the throne was not confirmed. The kingdom of France was divided in two. The road to Reims was also cut - and without a coronation in Reims there cannot be a King of France. Charles VII resided in the castle in Chinon, a great fortress consisting of three strongholds set in a row high above the River Vienne and surrounded by mighty walls. It was in this fortress, in 1429, that he was found by Joan, the Maid of Orleans who led him on the victorious epic journey to Reims and his coronation. Once Joan of Arc had fulfilled her short-lived destiny, she was abandoned by all and she spent part of the winter of 1429-1430 in the château at Sully-sur-Loire before setting off to join battle again. She was taken prisoner on 23rd May 1430.

The keep in Loches is another residence that belonged to "he who was almost king". It is an enormous keep for which he commissioned a number of defensive features. It was here that he accommodated his mistress, Agnès Sorel, making her one of the queen's ladies-in-waiting in 1444.

Agnès Sorel was a woman of outstanding beauty who led the way in court fashion. In Loches, her chef was none other than the famous Taillevent! Charles VII also stayed in Amboise occasionally, after confiscating the castle from the Vicomte de Thouars who was convicted of having plotting against Georges de La Trémoille, the king's favourite. Charles VII

ordered the strengthening of the system of defence. Throughout the 15th century, numerous castles and châteaux were built or renovated, among them Blancafort, Gien, La Verrerie, Maupas, Meillant, Menetou-Salon, Les Réaux, Montrésor, Ussé, Montsoreau, Brissac and the Château du Moulin. Charles VII died in 1461. He was succeeded by his son, Louis XI, who was born in 1423 in Loches where he was brought up. He then moved to Amboise in 1433 to live with his mother. After his coronation, Louis XI settled the queen in Amboise, a residence that was decidedly royal if lacking in sophistication. The king was constantly on the move. The birth of an heir, Charles, in 1470 struck fear into Louis XI's heart. He even went so far as to prohibit strangers from entering the town for fear that his son would contract the plague. The castle was a veritable fortress. The heir apparent's governor was Jean Bourré who was later to build the Château du Plessis-Bourré.

As to the king, he paid little attention to creature comforts. He was an inveterate traveller and hunter, always on the move. As long as he could keep control of his efficient system of administration through his messengers, he was happy to live frugally. He had no hesitation in staying in castles or châteaux that he happened upon in his travels or in meeting the lower classes.

He turned Loches into a state prison and commissioned the building of the castle in Langeais. Louis XI's favourite residence, however, was Plessis-lès-Tours, a small château which he purchased in 1463 and to which he added countless guardrooms since, with advancing years, his legendary mistrust became real paranoia.

It was in Amboise that the heir apparent married

Margaret of Austria in 1483 when he was aged thirteen. That same year, he succeeded Louis XI and took the title Charles VIII. He was married to Maximilian of Austria's daughter while still a child but, in 1491, he preferred Anne, heiress to the wealthy Duchy of Brittany,

Eels.

who had been married by proxy - to Maximilian of Austria! The wedding took place in Langeais but it was in Amboise, his birthplace, that the king wanted to commission a new building that would leave its mark. Thus it was that, in 1491, he incorporated into the Gothic construction architectural forms of Italian inspiration, a reminder of a campaign in Naples. The new castle in Amboise had no defences - it was a fine, but purely residential building. Charles VIII furnished it with luxury goods such as tapestries, Turkish carpets, and solid silver plate decorated with Anne of Brittany's cipher, a tressure. He returned from an expedition in Italy not only with some valuable objects which he placed in Amboise but also with artists and craftsmen.

In 1498 he hit his head on a lintel and died without leaving a male heir. The throne passed to his cousin, Louis XII, a descendant of Charles V. Louis XII divorced Joan of France, Louis XI's daughter, and married Anne of Brittany. He ordered the rebuilding of the castle in Blois, an Orléans family stronghold, using workers from the castle in Amboise. Again, the old castle was retained but an Italianate wing was added. Blois is a landmark in the development of the Renaissance style. Louis XII and Anne of Brittany had a large, luxurious Court. Anne was rich thanks to income from Brittany and from her other estates. In Blois, they enjoyed refinements such as "Oysters, Loire lampreys, trout, venison and pheasant, washed down with Burgundy wine".[1]

When Anne of Brittany died in 1514, two daughters from her numerous offspring were still alive. The elder one was Claude of France, who married François d'Angoulême, cousin to the king and heir to the throne which he mounted in 1515 after Louis XII's death. The younger daughter was Renée. Here, then, was Francis I, aged twenty. He had been brought up in Amboise where he set up court. In 1516, he summoned Leonardo da Vinci from Italy and settled him in Le Clos-Lucé, on the outskirts of the town of Amboise. Leonardo spent the last three years of his life there.

Francis I undertook new work in the castle in Amboise but his name is forever linked to Blois, which the queen preferred. From 1515 onwards, the Francis I Wing was built; it is one of the finest of all Renaissance constructions.

In 1519, Francis I launched a gigantic project - Chambord. Historian Ivan Cloulas has described Chambord as a "palace-city". The central section known as the "keep" is divided by two galleries laid out in the form of a cross to mark out four apartments on each floor. The double-spiral staircase stands at the centre of the cross and is said to be a simplified version of a quadruple spiral staircase designed by Leonardo da Vinci. Chambord is a huge residence but it was little used. The king came here only to hunt. His apartments were in a wing added on to the initial layout and were not completed until 1545.

During this period, a number of major châteaux were built or renovated:

Chenonceau, which was purchased in 1512 by Thomas Bohier, the husband of Catherine Briçonnet, was built from 1513 to 1517 on the site of a former manor house. A bridge was built over the Cher on the spot previously occupied by a mill. After the deaths of Thomas Bohier and his wife, the château became royal property.

Azay-le-Rideau, which was built between 1518 and 1527 for Gilles Berthelot, Treasurer of France, was constructed on piles and has only two wings instead of the four originally planned because, by 1527, the kingdom was on the verge of bankruptcy. Semblançay, General of Finances, was executed and Berthelot, who had connections with him, was forced to flee. Azay-le-Rideau was confiscated by the king. The building remained unfinished but that does not detract from the graceful harmony of this gem of Renaissance architecture.

La Bourdaisière in Montlouis was the residence of Philibert Babou, King's Counsellor. The monarch gave a donation to fund its extension.

Other châteaux from this period include Talcy, Villandry, Beauregard, Villesavin, Montreuil-Bellay and Serrant.

Francis I did not limit his building projects to the Loire Valley; he refurbished the château in Fontainebleau, the Louvre Palace, the château in Saint-Germain-en-Laye and many others.

Then came a period of misfortune. Queen Claude died in 1524. The king was in Italy where, having been defeated at the Battle of Pavia, he was taken prisoner by Emperor Charles V and removed to Spain. He stayed there for one year, only returning in 1526 after leaving his two sons as hostages in return for his own freedom.

In 1533, his son, Henry, married Catherine de Médicis. Henry's wife was destined to acquire fame;

his mistress, Diane de Poitiers, had already done so. Henry II mounted the throne in 1547. Amboise was used as the residence of the royal children.

Henry II gifted several estates to his mistress, Diane, including Chenonceau. She became fond of the château and she kept a watchful eye on the income from the vineyards and farms. A wonderful garden was laid out in 1551. Catherine de Médicis, her rival, purchased the château in Chaumont-sur-Loire in 1550 from a member of the La Rochefoucauld family. It was a large castle overlooking the Loire, rebuilt c. 1475.

Henry II died in 1559 and was succeeded by his son, Francis II. Catherine de Médicis soon ensured that her rival, Diane de Poitiers, who had lost her power and authority, was evicted from Chenonceau. Diane was forced to exchange Chenonceau for Chaumont, a castle which she never visited, preferring instead to retire to her beautiful Château d'Anet.

In 1560 the court left Blois and returned to Amboise. A conspiracy was afoot, led by the Protestants and by powerful noblemen opposed to the Duc de Guise. The conspiracy was discovered and repressed. Francis II, however, died that same year. Catherine de Médicis acted as regent for her second son, Charles IX, then aged ten. The period was troubled by the Wars of Religion. In 1572, the king's brother, Henry, was elected to the throne of Poland, and his sister, Margot, married Henry of Navarre, the future Henry IV. The marriage was designed to reconcile Protestants and Catholics but it ended in a blood-bath in Paris on 24th August 1572. The widescale slaughter of Huguenots was known as the St. Bartholomew's Day Massacre.

The court then left the Loire Valley and moved closer to Paris. Catherine de Médicis, however, continued to embellish Chenonceau.

Charles IX died in 1574. His brother, Henry III, returned from Poland to succeed him. He was faced with unrest and conspiracies. The coffers were empty and the days of major building projects were long gone. The castle in Angers was demolished. When Henry died in 1589, several months after Catherine de Médicis, the throne passed to Henry IV, King of Navarre, a descendant of St. Louis and the husband of Queen Margot, sister of the three previous kings. It took nine years of warfare, however, before he finally mounted the throne. The kings of France left the Loire Valley and the golden age of the châteaux was over. Several grand residences were nevertheless built after that time e.g. Cheverny from 1604 to 1634, Sully-sur-Loire, or Châteauneuf-sur-Loire. The French Revolution left a trail of damage. The château at Plessis-lès-Tours, among others, was almost totally demolished.

Amboise was used as a State prison for some time then suffered damage during the French Revolution. It is now the property of the Orléans family.

Langeais belongs to the Institut de France, Sully-sur-Loire to Loiret County Council and Châteauneuf-sur-Loire to the local council. Azay-le-Rideau has been State property since 1905, Chambord since 1930, Talcy since 1933 and Chaumont-sur-Loire since 1938.

These publicly-owned castles will not be mentioned again here. For the purposes of this book, we have sought to discover what gives privately-owned châteaux their special character and pinpoint the links created over the centuries with their occupants. Our selection is a random one and could have been different. There is no shortage of châteaux and castles along the banks of the Loire and all have a tale to tell. Here are just a few of those with the greatest interest in food.

1. *Ivan Cloulas:* La vie quotidienne dans les châteaux de la Loire au temps de la Renaissance. *Hachette*, 1983.

In a display case in the Château de La Ferté-Saint-Aubin.

*T*he cuisine of the châteaux could not have existed without the talented chefs and cooks who worked there. In homage, we have reproduced this letter, received last century from an enthusiastic chef presenting his apologies to the Marquis de Goulaine for being unable to enter his service.

To Monsieur le Marquis de Goulaine

Dear Sir,

I have received Monsieur le Marquis' telegram summoning me and deeply regret that I am unable to enter his service. This was the very employment I was seeking, in a house with an ancient aristocratic family to whom I could offer my culinary talents and live out the remainder of my life. Unfortunately, Man proposes and God disposes. Perhaps in the future, at a less distant time, I should be able to say to Monsieur le Marquis, "I am available for employment".

I am a Frenchman and a Breton. I am loyal to my word as I am to my sovereign. If, in the future, Monsieur le Marquis believes it right to summon me, then say so. Having fulfilled my obligations to my employers, I should be able to leave my post and come to serve Monsieur le Marquis. I have been hired and am taking up my position tomorrow morning with my wife, but shall I feel that such is my place? Perhaps Monsieur le Marquis will have his hunting season this winter, a season during which a culinary artist can reveal the full extent of his talents.

Like many other things, the culinary art survives thanks to the efforts of experienced professional chefs seeking to combat the decline of their species. As correspondent to L'Art Culinaire, I am attempting to breathe new life into this art form, the art of knowing how to cook and serve food, in short how to render a love of life. Unfortunately, I do not belong to the group for whom all doors have been opened. As a researcher who studies during the day, the passing of time leaves me insufficient freedom to undertake my research as I would wish.

May I one day find an employer who, like me, will be interested in the most sublime of all art forms and who will express a wish to assist me in my research. French cuisine is as useful worldwide as the rarest of all inventions.

I apologise, Monsieur le Marquis, for expressing myself at such great length in lines that I should not write.

I also apologise, Monsieur le Marquis, for my refusal to break a promise. I have given my word elsewhere. What else can I do?

I must wait.

I am, Sir, your most deeply respectful, humblest and devoted servant.

Signed: Gustave L...

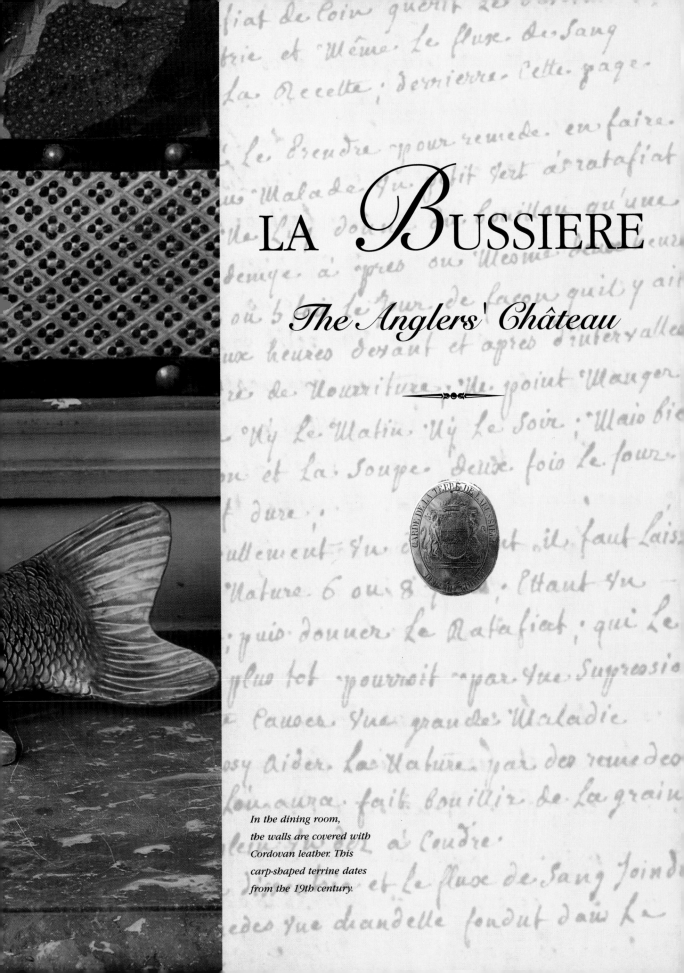

LA BUSSIERE

The Anglers' Château

*In the dining room,
the walls are covered with
Cordovan leather. This
carp-shaped terrine dates
from the 19th century.*

*L*a Bussière is known as the "Anglers' Château" because of its extensive collections, including a coelacanth, a rare reminder of prehistoric fauna, various moulds, glassware, paintings concerning the art of fishing, rods and large numbers of fishing flies. Moreover, La Bussière is reflected in the waters of a large lake created by Jean-Baptiste du Tillet during the reign of Louis XIV. At that time, the house was the focal point of a vast estate whose size is suggested by the dimensions of the barns built of pink brick with black diamond decoration that once contained the tithe from more than 30,000 hectares of land. The duTillet family owned the château from 1518 until the French Revolution. They commissioned the building of the present château during the reign of Louis XIII and had the grounds laid out by the famous landscape gardener, Le Nôtre.

The "Anglers' Château" is flanked by a large lake and a moat leading to the kitchen.

They emigrated and their château was confiscated. They were able to buy it back in the 19th century but were later obliged to sell it. For many years, it has been owned by the Chassevals, an old family from the Orléans area.

The kitchen overlooks the lake and still has its 16th-century brick walls. The most modern "appliance" in it is a huge coal-fired stove dating from the last century. Store rooms and pantries are used to stock the food for the large household. A bread oven and pump add the finishing touches to the château's self-sufficiency. The vegetable garden is particularly well-tended by the Comtesse de Chasseval who agreed to share her recipes with us and showed us a rare recipe book dating from 1761.

It is not often that we have the opportunity of reproducing recipe books dating from the 18th century. The one that Madame de Chasseval found for us is full of helpful hints and pharmaceutical prescriptions, which just goes to prove that cooking was also the basis for good health.

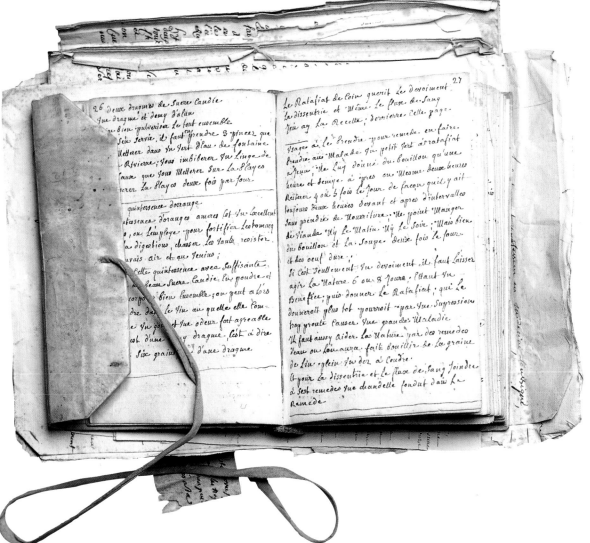

In the 1911-1912 season,
Auguste de Chasseval killed 382
pieces of game including
174 rabbits, 62 pheasant,
58 sandpipers and 2 plovers...
An average season
at the beginning of the century!

BROCHET
À L'ESTURGEON

Sturgeon-style pike

Wash the pike
well then slice into steaks.
Marinate for 4 to 5 hours
with fines herbes,
a little garlic, a little olive oil,
salt and pepper.
Quickly brown

the liver and heart and
place in a papillotte.
Lay the fish over the top.
Bake at a moderate heat.
Meanwhile, make a light
roux and add some
white wine.
Place the papillotte
on the serving dish and
pour the sauce over it.
(18th-century recipe).

FLAN DE POMMES DE TERRE SOUFFLÉ

Potato Soufflé

Cook eight potatoes then mash with a pestle and mortar. Pound a generous knob of butter with lemon peel or orange flower to flavour. Add eight egg yolks and mix well. Beat the egg whites until stiff as if making a sponge then blend into the remainder of the ingredients and cook. The soufflé should be sprinkled with sugar. (18th-century recipe).

CERISE COIFFÉE

Cherry Pyramid

Remove the stalks and stones from cherries and simmer in a light sugar and water syrup. Leave to cool then build up in layers as high as possible, crossing the cherries over. Add a stalk to the middle to form the fruit, sprinkle with castor sugar and dry in a kiln or in strong sunshine. (18th-century recipe).

BOUDIN À LA RICHELIEU

Richelieu Sausage

Take a good piece of boiled beef combining fat and lean meat. Pound well with a pestle and mortar then add some Spanish sauce and a knob of butter about the size of an egg. Mash together. Season with pepper, salt and nutmeg. Add two eggs, one after the other, and mix well (to achieve a smoother dish, pass through a sieve). Work the mixed ingredients in a bowl with a wooden spoon and set aside. Sprinkle with a little flour and roll out to a length of 5 cm (2 inches). Close off the ends of the "sausage" and sauté in a dish with clarified butter over a gentle heat.

Spanish Sauce

This is one of the great basic sauces which was in common use in the 19th and early 20th centuries. Given its complexity and more especially the time taken to prepare it, it has been simplified as much as possible. Nowadays, commercial meat stocks are an acceptable alternative.

Clarified Butter

Melt the butter and skim off the light-coloured part. Leave the whitish substance (casein) in the bottom of the pan. It is this which causes the butter to darken during cooking.

COQ EN PATE OU PIE DE POULET

Chicken Pie

Line a baking dish with flaky pastry. In the base of the dish, place some finely-chopped onion, chopped parsley and thin slices of bacon (fairly lean streaky is ideal). Lay pieces of chicken previously cooked in their own juices over the top. Add another layer of chopped onion and parsley, mashed cooked egg yolks, and a spoonful of finely chopped mushrooms. Pour over some good stock until the pieces of meat are well covered then add the flaky pastry "lid". Bake in a hot oven for 25 minutes. Cover the pie with buttered paper to ensure that the pastry does not burn when beginning to cook.

A ceramic fish made in Northern France. Below it is a 19th-century Italian salmon.

Œufs à la ouistiti

Coddled Eggs

Butter some small moulds and sprinkle with chopped parsley, salt and pepper. Break an egg into each mould. Place all the moulds in a large pan filled with hot water and put in the oven for 4 to 5 minutes. When the eggs are cooked, place them in a circle on a serving dish. Run a knife round the moulds to remove the eggs and serve with a sauce.

Sauce au gras

Mix a spoonful of flour, a knob of butter as big as an egg, salt and pepper and blend over the heat. Gradually add a bowl of meat stock. Pour over the eggs and serve hot.

Sauce au maigre

Mix a spoonful of flour, a knob of butter as big as an egg, salt and pepper and blend over the heat. Add caramel or any other colouring to the sauce as preferred. Gradually add some white wine and serve as above.

Potage à la royale

Royal Soup

Mix seven egg yolks and two egg whites with two ladles of cold, degreased meat stock. Place on a bain-marie and cook until thick without allowing to boil. Set aside to cool. When cold, cut into tiny pieces and pour the stock over it to serve. This recipe demands a chicken or beef stock, with vegetables from the garden, herbs and pepper. Simmer for at least 2 hours and leave to cool before degreasing. This type of stock is invaluable in cooking since it can be used in so many different recipes.

Bœuf carottes

Beef and Carrots

Take a good piece of chuck and insert pieces of fairly fatty bacon. Brown on all sides in olive oil. Reduce the heat and add a generous glass of white wine then cover and leave to simmer for 1 hour. Peel and chop two onions, six cloves of garlic with the green part removed, and a good kilo of sliced carrots. Once the beef has simmered for 1 hour, add the other ingredients and top up with more liquid (wine or water) if required, taking care not to add too much. Simmer for a further 1 1/2 hours on a very low heat. Check occasionally to ensure that the juices have not evaporated. Season with salt and pepper a few minutes before serving with potatoes cooked in their jackets and a good, crisp side salad with tarragon vinaigrette.

GLACE À LA VANILLE

Vanilla Ice Cream

1 litre milk
300 g castor sugar
8 or 10 egg yolks
1 vanilla pod

Bring the milk to the boil with the split vanilla pod. Put the egg yolks in a basin and whisk, gradually adding the sugar. Whisk for 10 minutes. When the milk boils, gradually pour onto the egg yolks. Place the mixture back on the heat and cook, slowly stirring with a wooden spoon.

The mixture is cooked:
- when the froth disappears
- when the mixture coats the spoon.

Remove from the heat and strain immediately through a fine-meshed sieve. Set aside in a basin. Prepare the mixture in the morning for an evening meal. When ready to freeze, add 25 cl of single cream then pour into the ice cream maker, cover and seal.

Stir until the ice cream is sufficiently stiff. If liked, add a little liqueur. The ice cream "takes" in 15 to 20 minutes. The cream is optional. If you do not have an ice cream maker, stir two or three times with a fork during freezing.

In La Bussière, jam is made in the old copper preserving pan and the recipes have changed very little since this one was written as follows in the 18th-century recipe books:

RECIPE FOR REDCURRANT JAM

Take one and a half pounds of sugar to one pound of fruit. Remove the pips from inside the redcurrants with a feather, taking care to crush and empty them. Leave about three or four inches of stalk. The syrup must be cooked so that it ? (illegible, perhaps reaches a rolling boil). When the syrup is cooked like this, add the redcurrants and when they swell, remove them from the heat then put them back again until they swell for the third time.

MENU for 28th October

White Nettle Soup
La Puisaye Style Stuffed Carp
Rum Baba

SOUPE AUX ORTIES BLANCHES

White Nettle Soup

This soup is prepared in the
same way as sorrel soup.
Drop the nettles into the butter,
add diced potato, and pour in
some water or, preferably,
chicken stock. Season with salt,
cover and simmer for 1 hour.
Blend the ingredients in an
electric blender and season with
pepper. Mix an egg yolk into
some cold stock and
add to the soup.

CARPE FARCIE À LA POYAUDINE

La Puisaye Style Stuffed Carp

For 4 people: Clean and trim a
large carp (approximately
1 kg) and wash for several
minutes under running water.
Drain then lay on a board and
stuff with a carefully-mixed
blend of 80 g lean, chopped
bacon, the carp liver, the roe
(if any), parsley, and shallot.
Add some white bread soaked in
milk, an egg, salt and pepper,
nutmeg and a few mushroom
stalks. Once the fish has been
filled with this stuffing, it is not
necessary to stitch it up
(although Madame de Chasseval
prefers to do so) if wrapped
in a wide, thin strip of pork fat
which is tied in place to hold
the fish and stuffing together.
Lay the fish in an ovenproof
dish and garnish with a dozen
spring onions previously

sweated in butter.
Add an equal number
of uncooked mushroom caps.
Pour on one glass of dry white
wine and bake in a hot oven for
20 minutes. To serve, remove
any remaining pork fat.
Deglaze with some crème
fraîche. It is preferable for the
mistress of the house to serve
the fish herself, to ensure
that each guest receives
an equal portion of fish,
stuffing, garnish and sauce.

BABA AU RHUM

Rum Baba

*This is a very easy and very
tasty recipe from an old lady
born in Martinique, who used
to supply the vintage rum.*

Beat one egg yolk with 90 g
sugar until white. Add a knob of
butter, a teaspoonful of baking
powder, three spoonfuls of milk
and 100 g flour. Beat the egg
white until stiff then blend into
the remaining ingredients.
Place the mixture in a buttered
ring mould and bake in a hot
oven. The baba is cooked when
springy to the touch. Remove
from the mould and leave to
cool. Decorate with glacé fruits
and imbibe with a sugar
and rum syrup.
Double the proportions
for a large baba.

LA FERTÉ SAINT-AUBIN

In the heart of Sologne

The kitchen in La Ferté-Saint-Aubin is filled with the scents of apples and pastries. It is preceded by a vast vaulted chamber leading into a dark wine cellar and the deep store rooms required by such a large household. Near the huge fireplace, in which a fire burns constantly, there is a bread oven, a cast-iron stove and countless strange utensils - copper pots, moulds, pewter jugs, and Pierrette's own preserves piled high on the shelves. She made us her own little madeleines, sponge cakes eaten straight from the oven.

However, in the heart of Sologne, an area famous for its game, people do not just eat desserts. River fish also have pride of place - carp, eels, pike etc. And there is, of course, game, the animals and birds that come from the private estates concealed behind wooden fences. Sologne does not reveal its secrets easily. The land is flat, dotted with lakes, thick coppices, and fields of short-stemmed maize. The height of the crop, though, is of little importance. It is grown for the wild boar and serves as a natural habitat for pheasants. There is water everywhere, forming lakes, canals or marshes. The towns are really large villages with cottages built of coloured brick. In the street, you will find the cloth-cap brigade and strutting hunters from Paris whose false air of timidity fools no-one. There are not many large châteaux in Sologne because of the dampness of the ground and the lack of quarries. La Ferté-Saint-Aubin is one of the most impressive. It stands on the site of an old fortress, on the banks of the Cosson which then flows on to Chambord. In the 16th century, the estate was inherited by the de Saint-Nectaire family (whose name was changed in registers of births, deaths and marriages to Senecterre then to Seneterre). François de Saint-Nectaire had a small château built; it was extended by his son, Henry. His grandson, Henry II, Maréchal de La Ferté-Senecterre during the reign of Louis XIV, commissioned the construction of the two large outbuildings lining the courtyard. The general layout, which would have involved demolishing the old château on the north side and flanking the main part of the building with two grandly projecting pavilions, is discernible today. In fact, one of the pavilions was built. As to the façade and outbuildings, they are representative of an amiable form of Classicism.

La Ferté was placed on the market several times and, for many years, remained in the hands of army men. The Maréchal de Lowendal (a descendant of the King of Denmark who served Austria, Denmark, Saxony, Russia and France in succession), one of the Talleyrands, then Prince Masséna, son of an imperial Maréchal, were among its owners. At that time, the estate covered an area of 5,000 hectares, with woodland,

The sugar loafs - and the sugar breaker.

farms and lakes. La Ferté was then purchased by an Irish family named O'Gorman who gave it some very strange neo-Gothic furniture. A section of the outbuildings was turned into an orphanage but fire broke out there in 1944. In short, the château was in a very poor state of repair when Jacques Guyot arrived in 1987. His first task was to undertake the restoration of the pavilion that had suffered fire damage. Since then, much repair and restoration work has been completed and still more is planned in order to keep up this large Classical house that was never finished.... the very feature that gives it its charm. Jean Renoir rightfully realised this when, in 1939, he used it to shoot the outdoor scenes in his film, *The Rules of the Game.*

The canalised R. Cosson flows round La Ferté, seen here from the rear.

*Coffee served in the main
18th-century drawing room. The
Maréchal de Lowendal brought this
impressive Murano glass chandelier
back from a military campaign.*

MADELEINES MINIATURES

Madeleine sponges

For 60 little cakes:

2 eggs, 10 g honey
90 g flour
1 pinch salt
10 g brown sugar
90 g melted butter
75 g castor sugar
1/2 tsp. baking powder

Mix the castor sugar, brown
sugar, salt, and eggs in a mixing
bowl. Beat well then add the
flour, cooled melted butter,
honey and baking powder.
Mix and leave in a cool place
for 30 minutes.
Fill the cake tins with an icing
bag or, if you do not have one,
with a spoon.
Bake in a moderate oven (Th. 6)
until cooked. The madeleines
are ready for eating
5 minutes later.
Leek Pie.

TOURTE AUX POIREAUX

Leek Pie

Make a rich shortcrust pastry by
mixing 500 g flour with 250 g
butter cut into small pieces until
it resembles fine breadcrumbs.
Then add two glasses of milk,
two egg yolks and season with
salt. Divide into two equal
portions, cover with a cloth
and set aside for 1 hour.
Take 800 g well-washed white
parts of leeks and chop finely.
Melt 40 g butter in a heavy-
bottomed sauté pan. Place the
leeks in the pan, cover and
leave to sweat gently for 30
minutes. Add 40 g flour, stir and
pour in 150 g milk and 150 g
cream. Mix then simmer
for 10 minutes. Add two
beaten eggs, stir and set aside.
Roll out the pastry.
Line a baking tin with one
portion of pastry, prick with
a fork and add the leek mixture
after seasoning with salt
and pepper. Cover with the
remainder of the pastry,
making a funnel in the middle.
Brush with egg yolk mixed with
a little milk.
Use any remaining pastry
to make diamond-shaped
decorations and lay out
in a flower shape around
the funnel. Bake in a hot oven
until the pastry is cooked and
golden brown.

*A wild boar ready to be cut up
in the basement kitchen.*

GALETTES
DE POMMES DE TERRE

Potato Cakes

Cook 200 g potatoes, mash and add 200 g flour, 100 g melted butter and 2 eggs. Mix well, pour into a round dish, mark out in squares with a fork and bake for 20 minutes. Serve with crème fraîche. This potato cake is also called a "*truffiat*" or a "*bourre-chrétien*" (literally, "Stuff-a-Christian").

ANGUILLE
À LA POULETTE

Braised Eel

Skin and clean a large eel. Cut into 5 cm (2-inch) pieces. Leave to disgorge for a few hours in cold water then blanch. Melt 50 g butter in a large sauté pan. Add an equal quantity of flour, mix and pour on 1 litre boiling liquid consisting of one-half white wine and one-half fish or other stock. Blend the sauce until smooth then add the pieces of eel, a few small spring onions, a bouquet garni, some salt and pepper. When the eel and onions are cooked, lay out on a serving dish and sieve the sauce. Quickly blend with 3 egg yolks and pour over the eel. Serve with golden brown croûtons and mushrooms sweated in butter.

CONSERVES
DE CITRONS CONFITS

Lemon Preserves

Take some untreated lemons, if available. If not, wash and brush the lemons well under running water. Cut in half widthways then cut each half into four without slicing right through the rind. The quarters should remain joined at the base. Place in a jar and cover with kitchen salt. Leave to marinate for 3 or 4 days then rinse well and drain. Place in jars and cover with olive oil. Seal the jars and store. Lemon preserves are used in North African cookery and in recipes such as chicken and lemon. The lemon-flavoured olive oil can also be used in cooking and in vinaigrettes.

Potato Cake.

TARTE TATIN

Upside-down Apple Tart

Make shortcrust pastry with 250 g flour, 125 g softened unsalted butter, 1 pinch salt and 1 generous spoonful of double cream. Set aside for 30 minutes. Melt some butter and sugar in the base of a sponge tin. Add 1.3 kg of dessert apples cut into quarters. Brown in the butter, adding butter and sugar if necessary to ensure that the apples caramelise. Place the shortcrust pastry over the top and push the edges down into the tin. Bake in a hot oven until the pastry is cooked. Turn out onto a round serving dish and serve immediately with whipped cream. Tarte Tatin is the pride and joy of the Sologne area. It is undoubtedly the most successful "failure" in culinary history, which is not short of near disasters! Early in this century, the Misses Tatin owned the Hôtel Tatin et Terminus opposite the railway station in Lamotte-Beuvron. If the culinary brotherhood known as the Confrérie de Lichonneux, upholders of tradition if ever there were, is to be believed, the hotel was rushed off its feet one day and one of the two sisters concoted a dessert which was neither a tart nor a form of baked apple. She placed the quartered apples and some sugar in a buttered cake tin, covered them with pastry and put the "tart" in the oven. Another version of her invention was much less dramatic. The two sisters had no oven and therefore made their apple tart directly on the top of their stove. The result was usually burnt! Hence the idea of putting the tart upside down in a cake tin before it was cooked. The Confrérie de Lichonneux de Tarte Tatin prohibits the use of cream or jam in the tart and is against any use of spirits to set it alight. However, far from Sologne, it has often been adorned and transformed by the imagination of other chefs.

A Sologne Menu

SOUPE DE CHÂTAIGNES

Chestnut Soup

1 kg chestnuts, 55 g butter, the whites of 4 leeks (well-cleaned and finely chopped), 4 carrots (peeled and chopped), 4 turnips (peeled and chopped), 1 potato (peeled and chopped), 3 tbsp. crème fraîche, salt, freshly-ground pepper.

Slash the husk of the chestnuts and place in a saucepan. Cover with water, bring to the boil and simmer for 10 minutes. Drain then peel the chestnuts while still hot. If they cool too quickly, place them back in boiling water again so that they are easier to peel. They can also be cut in two and the nut can then be removed with a spoon.

Melt the butter in a pan and add the chopped leeks. Sweat for 10 minutes then add the other vegetables and chestnuts. Season with salt and pepper. Add 2 litres water. Cover and bring to the boil. Simmer for 45 minutes. Puree the vegetables in a blender. Check the seasoning. Blend in some crème fraîche and serve. The region has had a traditional ceremony since the 8th century known as the "Fête aux Châts". The festivities are in honour of the chestnut.

FAISAN À LA COMPOTE DE COINGS

Pheasant with Quince Compote

After the hunt, hang the unplucked pheasant in a cool place. When it is to be cooked, pluck and draw it, then flame it and set aside the cleaned liver. Make some stuffing with the liver, a small quantity of finely-chopped bacon, shallots, parsley, salt and pepper. Fill the cavity with the stuffing.
Place a few slices of fairly fatty bacon in a casserole with sliced carrots, onion rings, a bouquet garni, and two cloves. Lay the pheasant on top and pour

This majestic sink and splashback, made from a single block of marble, has been in the pantry since the 18th century.

on 50 cl white wine and an equal quantity of chicken or other stock. Cover with bacon and cook in a very cool oven for 4 hours. While the pheasant is cooking, wash a few quince, cut into quarters, remove the core and place them in a pan of boiling water for 5 minutes. Drain, rinse under cold water and peel. Put an adequate quantity of sugar into a pan with some lemon juice and finish cooking the quince.

Place the fruit on a compote dish and reduce the syrup. Pour over the quince and serve with the pheasant.

When the pheasant is cooked, remove from the casserole and cut into pieces. Skim off the top cooking fat and pour the base over the pheasant.

The bread oven next to the fireplace in the kitchen.

L'ÉTANG SOLOGNOT DE LÉONE

A recipe known to the women of Sologne. This one was handed down by Léone to her daughter, Micheline, in La Ferté-Saint-Aubin

Serves 6: Lay 6 slices of fruit cake in the bottom of a fireproof dish.
Pour on 8 tbsp. of water and 3 tbsp. of rum. Cook over a moderate heat for 5 minutes.
Bring 50 cl milk to the boil with a deseeded vanilla pod.
Beat 4 egg yolks with 100 g sugar and 2 level tbsp. of cornflour. Gradually pour on the milk and thicken over a low heat, stirring all the time. Bring to the boil.
Pour this fairly thick custard over the slices of fruit cake.
Beat the egg whites until stiff then carefully blend in 75 g castor sugar.
Place spoonfuls of meringue on the custard, sprinkle with sugar and bake for 15 minutes until golden.
Serve cold.

A rare 17th-century spoon.

26 | 27

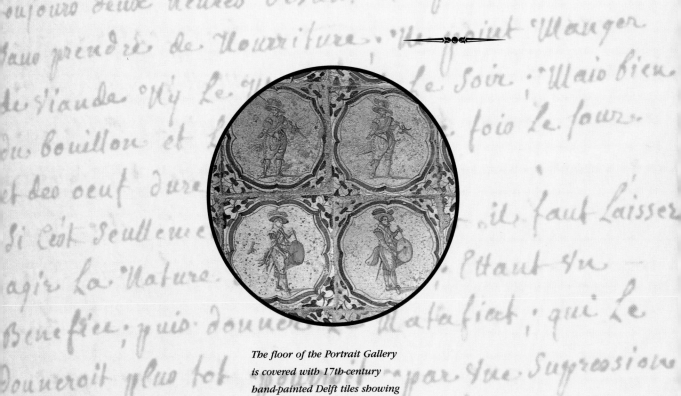

BEAUREGARD

Under the watchful eye of history

The floor of the Portrait Gallery is covered with 17th-century hand-painted Delft tiles showing an army on the move. The inventory lists 1,152 horsemen, 1,584 musketeers, 1,360 pikemen, 60 drummers etc. In all, there are more than 5,000 tiles.

The equestrian portrait of Henry IV has pride of place among the 327 famous people in the portrait gallery in the Château de Beauregard, an elegant 16th-century residence listed as a historic monument by Mérimée in the 19th century. The portraits were commissioned by Paul Ardier, former minister to the crown, to decorate the long Renaissance gallery that linked the two wings. This was not the only portrait gallery of the day; there is another one in the Medici Gallery in Florence. The one in Beauregard, however, is particularly important. It was carefully prepared, as indicated in the *Livre des Eloges*, a work also kept in the château which indicates, for each portrait, the sources consulted. The portraits are grouped per reign of the kings of France, from Philip VI de Valois to Louis XIII. There are, of course, leading political figures but there are also foreign monarchs, scientists and writers. The gallery in Beauregard is richly decorated with allegories and is a delight to the eye, as well as being a mine of information for historians.

The private dining room in Beauregard.

The château contains other treasures such as the "Bell Cabinet", valuable furniture, a Dutch cartel with carillon which plays dance tunes on the hours and, of course, a kitchen which was still in use until recent times. It is occupied by Comtesse Alain de Cheyron du Pavillon whose family purchased it in 1925. Before then, it had had a series of owners since its sale by the Ardier family in 1825.

LA POULE AU POT D'HENRI IV

Henry IV's Chicken Stew

During the reign of Henry IV, vegetable gardens were already full of different types of vegetable. Most of them still exist and others have been added since, including of course the potato which appeared only two hundred years later. However, artichokes, parsnips, carrots, cabbages, turnips and leeks had already existed for many years...

To make a good chicken stew, you need a good plump free range chicken for boiling. Remove the liver and gizzard then split the gizzard in two to clean it of grit. You will also need a Parma-style ham from which you should set aside the fat each time you take off a slice. You will need dry bread, one week old, and some good eggs like the ones we used to eat. Not to mention some good brandy from your private cellar. It is ideal if you have to hand various garden herbs such as parsley, tarragon, chives, sage, chervil etc.

Put a large pan of cold water to boil with some coarse salt. Meanwhile, mix together the fat from the ham, the crumbs from the bread soaked in milk then squeezed dry, a few beaten eggs,

the cleaned liver and the gizzard. Use sausagemeat for additional volume if there is not much fat from the ham. Mix all the ingredients and add any herbs available. You can also add chopped onion and garlic crushed with the flat of your hand. The mixture has to be compact and smooth. Add a glass of brandy, a very little salt and a large amount of pepper, ensuring that the ingredients remain well-balanced. To check on the taste, remove a small piece of stuffing and fry in a small quantity of butter over a low heat. Taste, then adjust seasoning as required. The stuffing is ready.

Of course, you have to stuff the boiling fowl but set some stuffing aside to fill some cabbage leaves as a garnish for the chicken stew.

Stuff the chicken and stitch up. When the water boils, place the chicken in it, turn down the heat and leave to simmer gently for 1 hour. Then add all the peeled, chopped vegetables (carrots, turnips, leeks, swedes, celery, onions stuck with cloves, and cabbage). Before placing the cabbage in the pot, remove the best outer leaves and blanch for approximately 2 minutes. Leave the boiler and vegetables to simmer gently for a further 1 hour.

Meanwhile, take the blanched cabbage leaves. Place spoonfuls of stuffing on the leaves and tie into parcels (1 per guest). Add to the pot 20 minutes before the end of the cooking time.

When everything is cooked, make a roux of one-half butter and one-half flour, letting it turn golden but not brown. Then add a few ladles of stock, stirring continuously. Simmer over a low heat until the sauce begins to thicken. Add some cream to lighten, or an egg yolk beaten with some slightly cooled stock and a drop of vinegar.

Remove the chicken and the well-drained vegetables. There must be only a drop of water left in the vegetables or even none at all. Lay the pieces of chicken out on a large serving dish with the stuffing cut into slices. Garnish with the vegetables and stuffed cabbage leave.

Serve the sauce in a sauce boat.

The main kitchen in Beauregard. The central table encircles a load-bearing pillar. The fireplace is decorated with a saying dated 1527, "Keep your promise to those to whom you had made it".

SALADE BEAUREGARD

Beauregard Salad

This "salad" is really
a mosaic of appetisers
on a bed of lamb's tongue
lettuce. 500 g fresh
chopped mushrooms
in a vinaigrette containing
tuna fish flakes. 1 kg cooked,
shelled prawns with 3 diced
tomatoes. Black olives served
with an olive oil mayonnaise.
150 g Roquefort cheese and
100 g walnut kernels with
a walnut oil vinaigrette.
8 slices Grisons meat and diced
croûtons rubbed with garlic
served in a traditional
vinaigrette. One lettuce
and palm tree hearts split
lengthways served with a
mustard, olive oil and shallot
vinaigrette. 4 slices smoked
salmon or the equivalent
in offcuts with a lemon and
cream sauce. 4 halved mature
goats' cheeses laid on a slice
of bread and lightly toasted
in the oven, served
with a traditional vinaigrette.
4 slices foie gras on lambs'
tongue lettuce moistened
with a very mild vinaigrette.
For 4 people, allow
300 g lambs' tongue lettuce.

FLAMICHE AUX POIREAUX

Leek Pie

Serves 5 to 6

Peel and finely chop 500 g
leeks, using all the white part
but only some of the green section. Place in a pan to sweat
with 50 g butter. Gradually add
a further 50 g butter as they
cook. Pour in 1 tablespoon
water to soften the leek,
cover and simmer gently until
the leek has become very soft
and all the liquid has been
absorbed. Add a quantity
of crème fraîche equivalent
to one-quarter of the weight
of cooked leeks and season
well. Divide 500 g puff pastry
into two. Roll out one half
on a damp pastry board
to form a round. Place the leeks
in the middle, leaving 3 cm -
1 1/2 inches round the edge.
Brush the edge with water.
Lay the second half of the
pastry, rolled out in the same
way, over the top pressing it
down with your fingers onto the
damp section of the bottom
layer to ensure that the two
rounds of pastry are well sealed.
Slash the edge to help the pastry
to rise during baking and indent
with a knife. Brush the surface
with an egg yolk diluted with a
drop of water then mark out the
surface with a knife.
Bake in a hot oven for
10 minutes then reduce
to a moderate heat and bake
for a further 30 minutes.
The surface should be golden
brown. Serve very hot.

PAIN DE JAMBON

Ham Loaf

One of Anne-Marie de Pavillon's recipes for a light evening meal.

Mix 6 egg yolks, 250 g chopped ham and 250 g grated gruyere cheese to make a thick, smooth paste. Beat the egg whites until very stiff and fold them into the mixture as you would for a soufflé. Pour into a buttered loaf tin or charlotte mould and smooth the top with a wooden spoon or spatula. Bake in a bain-marie in a moderate oven until the "loaf" is cooked and golden.

Sauce

Stir 30 g butter and 30 g flour over a gentle heat until it thickens and become frothy. Pour in 40 cl hot water and mix, stirring all the time. Bring back to the boil and add 2 tsp. tomato puree then season with salt and pepper.

PINTADE BRAISÉE AUX ENDIVES

Braised Guinea Fowl with Chicory

Cut a good-sized guinea fowl into eight pieces and dust with flour. Clean 600 g chicory and cut in eight lengthways. Finely chop 50 g best back or lean streaky bacon. Melt 30 g butter in a pan over a low heat. Fry the pieces of guinea fowl until golden then add the bacon. Simmer over a low heat for 10 minutes, turning the pieces of poultry frequently. Discard the fat that runs off during the cooking. Pour in 3 spoonfuls of Muscat wine and turn the pieces of guinea fowl over in the wine. Leave until the liquid has evaporated. Add the chicory, cover and leave until light golden brown, turning often.

This takes approximately 15 minutes. Add 150 g crème fraîche, a pinch of nutmeg and some pepper. Leave to reduce over a low heat for 15 minutes until the sauce coats the pieces of meat then add the juice of 1 lemon, mix and serve immediately. To garnish the dish with chicory, allow 3 lbs. chicory. Cook in a separate pan until golden brown and add to the guinea fowl as soon as they have become soft. Add a pinch of cornflour to prevent the cream from curdling.

These Gien plates were painted c. 1920 by Madame de Gosselin, Madame de Pavillon's grandmother. They are used for family meals and echo the subject matter on the tiles in the Portrait Gallery.

Amy's Apple Charlotte.

CURRY DE PORC AU CIDRE

Pork Curry in Cider

Cut 1.2 kg pork loin into 2 cm - 1 inch cubes. Peel and slice five onions. Heat 1 tsp. oil with 20 g butter. Cook the pieces of meat over a high heat until golden brown on all sides then lower the heat and dust lightly with flour. Stir well, add the onions and leave to colour slightly. Dust the meat and onions with a good sprinkling of curry powder and pour on two glasses of dry cider. Stir, add a bouquet garni and leave to cook over a low heat for approximately 1 1/2 hours. Check the cooking juices and, if necessary, add a little more cider.

Peel 1 kg russet apples, chop into cubes and cook in a little butter until golden brown, stirring from time to time. When the apples are cooked, season with salt and pepper and add 150 g crème fraîche. Leave to boil for 5 minutes. Lay the meat out on the serving dish, put the golden apples round the edge, and pour on the curry sauce. The quantity of curry powder used depends on personal taste. Serve this dish with well-flavoured rice such as thai or basmati.

GRATIN DE POIRES

Pear Gratin

Serves 6: Use a 1 kg tin of pears in syrup. Butter some ovenproof porcelain dishes. Place a pear half in each dish. Mix 120 g castor sugar with three egg yolks and beat until white. Add the blanched zest of half an orange, 50 g ground almonds and 30 g butter. Mix well then pour in 10 cl milk and 10 cl cream. When the mixture is smooth, pour over the pears and place in a preheated oven. Cook on thermostat 6 until golden brown. Serve warm but not hot.

CHARLOTTE AMY

Amy's Apple Charlotte

An old recipe given to us by Amy, a British friend. Serves 6.
Approximately 2 kg apples (a slightly acid variety if possible), the rind of an orange, breadcrumbs, butter, cinnamon, sugar, and sultanas (optional). Butter a charlotte tin well and dust with breadcrumbs. Cut the apples into very thin slices. Put a thick layer in the tin, dust with cinnamon, sugar and breadcrumbs. Add a few small knobs of butter and a few tiny pieces of orange rind (and sultanas if used). Push down well, then add another layer of apples and repeat the operation, ending with a layer of breadcrumbs. Bake in a cool oven for approximately 1 1/2 hours. Leave to get cold before removing from the tin and serve with double cream or custard. The dessert can also be warmed through in a moderate oven before serving. It's delicious.

GÂTEAU MANOLITO

Manolito Cake

Beat four eggs with a tin of condensed milk, the same quantity of ordinary milk and 125 g grated coconut. Run some caramel round the edges and base of a tin and cook in a bain-marie. To ensure that the coconut blends into the cream well, beat regularly while cooking otherwise it sinks to the bottom. Then bake in a moderate oven for approximately 30 minutes. This cake can be made the day before it is needed.

The kitchen. The corbelled working surface
is typical of the Loire Valley.

CHENONCEAU

The ever-present Diane

This is not a royal residence but it was the residence of queens and the name of Chenonceau immediately conjures up images of graceful living, serenity and pleasure enjoyed by a court that was constantly on the move. For four hundred years the River Cher has been flowing beneath the arches of the most beautiful castle-bridge in the world without causing any damage. Yet beautiful though the well-known picture of Chenonceau may be, this is nothing compared to the joy of visiting the interior, going down to the kitchens and back up to the piano nobile, strolling along the long gallery, and finally going upstairs to the striking bedchamber of Queen Louise, a monarch for ever in mourning. Chenonceau is not a very large château but it is difficult to leave it. Nevertheless Diane de Poitiers, mistress of King Henry II, was forced to give it to Catherine de Médicis in exchange for the Château de Chaumont which she never visited after her lover's death.

It was Diane who commissioned the garden laid out on the banks of the Cher. Chenonceau was a gift from the king (to avoid any risk of her property being taken from her, she had the estate placed on the market and repurchased it) who had received it from his father. He had confiscated it from Antoine Bohier, one of the kingdom's leading financiers. The Bohiers commissioned the building of the château on the site of the Marques' residence of which only one tower has survived. This was one of the earliest examples of French Renaissance architecture, and one of the most successful. Diane de Poitiers enthusiastically set about developing her estate. She extended the vineyard (an inventory carried out by her noted the presence, in the cellars, of "twelve casks of wine from plants brought from Beaune, Anjou, Orléans and Arbois and grown on the Chenonceau estate"). It was she who purchased the land at Chisseaux, she who ordered the laying out of gardens and vegetable gardens, and she who commissioned

In Chenonceau, the kitchens are in one of the pillars of the bridge. Food was landed at a small pontoon on the R. Cher.

Philibert de l'Orme to build a bridge across the Cher. The entwined initials of the two lovers are included in much of the château's decoration. After the king's death, Catherine de Médicis evicted her rival and, having taken over Chenonceau, continued with the work that Diane had begun. She ordered new gardens, hosted sumptuous entertainments, and commissioned the building of the gallery over the river which had already been planned before her arrival. It would be more accurate to say "the galleries" because there are two of them, one above the other, with an attic storey at the very top. However, the ethereal architecture ensured that the building retained all the lightness of a bridge.

When Catherine died, it was Queen Louise, widow of Henry III and the sad "wife in love with a man who loves only men", who inhe-

One of Bernard Voisin's purchases for Chenonceau was this fine old drawing. It is part of the château's collection of plans and picturesque illustrations, including a set of plans from the 19th century showing the intention to demolish the gallery over the R. Cher. Luckily, this aesthetic outrage was never committed. The drawing can be dated after 1559 since it shows the bridge, but before 1576 since the gallery has not yet been built.

rited the château. She lived there dressed in white, the colour of royal mourning, "in the sepulchral setting that she wanted", writes Bernard Voisin.

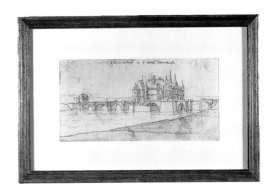

Chenonceau passed out of the limelight. Some work was carried out in the 17th century, Louis XIV made a brief visit, then the château was sold, in 1733, to the Farmer General, Dupin. Madame Dupin is remembered as a patron of arts and letters, and as a good hostess. Jean-Jacques Rousseau declared, "There was much amusement in this beautiful setting, and the food was good. I became as fat as a monk there!"

After Madame Dupin, Chenonceau was less well-tended and it began to lack lustre. Madame Pelouze, who purchased the château in 1864, envisaged the demolition of the gallery but did not go ahead with her plans. Then the château was repossessed after a bankruptcy and sold at auction in 1913 to Henri Menier, a rich industrialist whose family still owns it today. It is Bernard Voisin, Curator of Chenonceau since 1952, who has made the castle of queens so well-known to the public and it was he who met us for the purposes of this book, cooking being an essential part of the history of good food. We hope that Diane de Poitiers would have appreciated these recipes.

HATELETS DE BOUDIN BLANC À LA CHAIR DE CHAPON ET DE BOUDIN NOIR

White and Black Sausage Kebabs

Black and white were the colours of Diane de Poitiers

Black Sausage

Dice 2 kg onions, blanch them in boiling water to remove the strong taste, drain them and fry them in 1/2 lb. lard without allowing to brown. Dice 1 kg well-cleaned hog's fat. Chop some parsley. Add the hog's fat and parsley to the onions with 250 g cream.

Mix in 2 litres pig's blood, salt, pepper and spices to taste. Prepare the sausage skins: wash and scrape the gut well then blow through it to ensure that it is not punctured. Knot off one end then force the mixture through a funnel to fill the skin. Separate each sausage at the required length (in this case, they are small). Bring a pan of water to the boil, lay in the black sausages and leave them to cook for 45 minutes without allowing to boil. Prick the sausages to check whether they are cooked - if any blood runs out, they require more time. When they are ready, remove from the water, place on a clean cloth and rub with a piece of fatty bacon to make them shine.

White Sausage

Take the meat from the breast of a capon or any other roasted poultry and an equal quantity of chopped veal udder or cooked hog's fat. Soak some white bread in milk until it has completely soaked up the liquid, season with salt and dry over a high heat until it comes away from the bottom of the pan. Add to the chopped meat. There must be equal quantities of all the ingredients to make good sausagemeat. Mix in six egg yolks beaten with two spoonfuls of cream. Chop the onions, blanch in boiling milk then drain and fry in lard until golden. Meanwhile, sieve the sausagemeat, then mix with the onions and season with salt, pepper and nutmeg. Fill the skin in the same way as for the black sausage and cook in milk. Put alternating black and white sausages on skewers and grill gently.

Right:
The original floor tiling (1521)
decorated with the fleur-de-lys
in the bedrooms
on the first floor.

Dos de Sandre
« Marie Stuart »

Fillet of Pike-Perch
à la Mary, Queen of Scots

Serves 6: Lift off six fillets
of pike-perch weighing
approximately 150 g each.
Lightly sweat a julienne
of courgettes, six deseeded
tomatoes reduced in olive oil,
and season with salt
and pepper.

Sauce

Chop a shallot. Reduce in 20 cl
dry wine and a drop
of raspberry vinegar,
then blend in two spoonfuls
crème fraîche and add 350 g
butter. Season with salt and add
a pinch of cayenne pepper.

To serve

Lay the fillet of pike-perch
on a plate, cover with the tomato, pour on the sauce then
add the julienne of courgettes
and sprinkle with
chopped chives.

Aspic de foie gras

Foie Gras in Aspic

*Foie Gras in Aspic served in the
bedchamber of the five queens*

Cut 50 g pieces out of a goose
liver. Pour a little jelly made
with sparkling Vin de Vouvray
in the base of small moulds,
lay the rounded pieces of foie
gras over the top, place a thin
slice of truffle on each one
and cover with jelly. Put in a
cool place until the jelly has set
then remove from moulds.

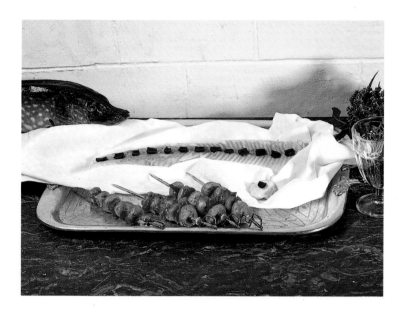

*The vineyard in Chenonceau
produces Touraine wine of all three
colours. The vinification process
is carried out in the small village
next to the château. On the right
is the pump that used to supply
the château with its water.
The number of hooks is indicative
of the size of the kitchen.
Below is a huge stove built
in a room in one of the piles of the
bridges. It was used during the First
World War when Gaston Menier
turned Chenonceau into a hospital.
Two thousand wounded soldiers
were given care and shelter here.*

BROCHET DU CHER

River Pike

The bone structure
of a pike makes it difficult
to lift off fillets. Instead,
cook it whole and divide
it when serving.
Gut the fish by the gills,
without slitting it open.
Tie up the head and place
in a fish kettle with the stock
described below, a handful
of salt and some coarsely-ground
pepper.

Fish stock

Two-thirds water for one-third
dry white wine, a few slices
of lemon, some thyme, bay,
and a few peppercorns.
sprigs of parsley and some
celery. Simmer the ingredients
for 1 hour.
Lay the pike in the stock,
cover and cook over a low heat
for 30 minutes, or longer depending on the size of the fish.

Check with the point
of a knife or pull a fin.
If it comes away easily,
the fish is cooked.
Meanwhile, brush a truffle until
clean. Cut into thin slices
and sweat them in a small
quantity of water.
Remove the pike from
the fish kettle. Filter the stock
and make a roux with half
butter and half flour.
Pour on the stock, whisk,
leave to cook and add a few
tiny pieces of truffle.
Skin the pike and carefully lift
off the fillets.
Lay on a white cloth and add
the slices of truffle.
Remember that the cheeks are
delicious.
Serve with the white sauce
containing the tiny
pieces of truffle.
After removing the fillets,
keep the remainder
of the flesh to make quenelles.

GELINE DE TOURAINE FORESTIÈRE « LA DAME NOIRE »

Chicken with Mushrooms

Take a plump "dame noire"
chicken, cut into pieces
and season with salt
and pepper.
Fry in a pan, add four large
shallots, flambé
with Marc de Touraine,
then deglaze with a dry white
wine from the Château
de Chenonceau.
Cover and simmer gently
for 1 hour.
Fry 150 g diced bacon in duck
fat, add 500 g baby potatoes
and 300 g oyster mushrooms.
At the end of the cooking time,
place the garnish around the
chicken, simmer for a further
15 minutes and serve simply
sprinkled with chopped chives
and chervil.

BOUCHÉES DE DIANE

Diane vol-au-vents

Take one partridge for 4 guests.
Melt 150 g butter and add
a finely-chopped mirepoix
as follows:

100 g carrots
80 g onions
parsley stalks
fragments of thyme
chopped bay leaves

Remove the meat from
the previously-cooked partridges
and set aside.
Add the skin and bones to the
mirepoix and pour on:

30 cl vinegar
20 cl white wine

Leave to reduce completely.
Then add:

1 litre Spanish sauce
2 litres game stock
1 litre marinade

Cover and leave to simmer
gently for 4 hours.
Add a few peppercorns.
Strain the sauce through
a sieve, pressing the ingredients.
Add some game stock
and marinade and reduce again
to obtain 1 litre of liquid.
Strain through a fine sieve.
Whip 20 cl cream and add
to the sauce with a few pieces
of truffle and a few chopped
whites of hard-boiled eggs
to give the colours
of Diane de Poitiers
(black and white).
Cut the partridge meat
into small cubes and fill
vol-au-vent cases.
Pour over the Diane sauce
and heat in the oven.

BEIGNETS DE CULS D'ARTICHAUTS

Artichoke Heart Fritters

It was Catherine de Médicis
who had the first artichokes
imported, as she did so many
other novelties that marked
the period of the Renaissance,
among them vegetables such
as beans, recipes such as
marzipan, and of course
the fork which then had two
prongs. Cook eight artichokes
and cool in cold water.
Set aside the leaves for another
dish and remove the straw.
Set the hearts aside.
In a bowl, place six spoonfuls
flour, two spoonfuls oil,
two eggs, one spoonful vinegar,
half-a-glass of beer, salt and
pepper. Add the artichokes
and mix well.
Put the artichoke fritters
into a deep fat fryer filled
with boiling oil so that they crisp
up immediately.
When they are golden,
drain and place on a towel
with fried parsley.

GÂTEAU AU CHOCOLAT

Chocolate Cake

In a bain-marie, melt
300 g dark cooking chocolate
with 300 g unsalted butter.
When the mixture is smooth,
add two spoonfuls crème fraîche
and set aside. Beat six egg yolks
with 100 g sugar until white.
Add to the chocolate mixture
and beat well. Beat five egg
whites until stiff then fold into
the chocolate mixture. Set
one-third aside as topping.
Carefully fold in 100 g sieved
flour then pour into a greased,
floured cake tin. Ensure that you
have already heated the oven.
Bake in a moderate oven,
checking to ensure that the cake
does not overcook. When the
cake is cooked, leave to cool
and cut in two through the
middle. Spread with some of the
mixture set aside, sandwich the
cake together again and spread
the top with the remainder
of the mousse. Decorate
with walnuts, other fruit
or whipped cream.

VILLANDRY

A passion for beauty

*T*he gardens in Villandry are a sheer delight, enthusiasti-cally tended by Henri Carvallo, Curator of the château which his great-grandfather, Joachim, purchased in 1906 with a view to restoring it. At that time, Villandry was on the point of being demolished, having been disfigured by additions, by the fake windows that had spoiled its façades, by the walling-up of the arches round the main courtyard and by the filling in of its moat. Beneath the English-style gardens laid out in the 19th century, Joachim Carvallo could imagine the original designs and the harmonious Renaissance architecture. He therefore abandoned a brilliant scientific career to

devote himself to the restoration of Villandry and, later, to a passionate crusade to save historic buildings throughout France, founding the *Association de la Demeure Historique*. His task was never-ending, for France has so many historic buildings that have to be saved from the damage of passing years or brought back from oblivion. In Villandry, however, he succeeded - superbly!

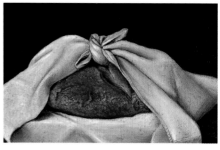

Villandry was built by Jean Le Breton, Minister of Finance during the reign of Francis I, on the site of an old fortress of which one square tower has survived. The château is known to have been completed c. 1536, which means that it dates back to the end of the Renaissance. No reference was made to the feudal era; instead, there were open courtyards, colonnades and gardens, and an openness in the design of the frontages that paved the way for Classicism. The château remained in the same family until the 18th century then the Castellanes, a great family from Provence, refurbished the interior and ordered the construction of the vast Classical outbuildings.

*Opposite:
This engraving
shows the condition
of the château when
it was owned by Baron
Hainguerlot
in the 19th century.
Below: Country Loaf,
a small painting by the
Zurburan School.*

Joachim Carvallo sought, throughout his life, to give Villandry back the grace and spiritual harmony that it had enjoyed when it was first built. He also added countless works of art. The memoirs written by his daughter, Guitte, helped us to retrace his recipes, blending the fire of Spanish cooking with the gentle cuisine of the Touraine region.

*The dining room
in Villandry.*

Joachim CARVALLO'S Hispano-Moorish menu

Joachim Carvallo was a strict man. He was also a man of principles - and he applied them to his crusade in defence of historic buildings, to the upbringing of his children, and to the production of good food. From the book of memoirs written by his daughter, Guitte Carvallo, among other recipes for "mouthwatering creations capable of becoming like the spiritual soul of a prayer", we have taken this equally tasty tale.

When the Carvallo family was on holiday in the Auvergne, they visited a fine mediaeval castle. Joachim Carvallo decided to encourage the owner to join the *Association de la Demeure Historique* and they were duly invited to lunch. It was doubtless a good meal, but not good enough for Joachim who declared, "Madam, allow me to cook you a meal worthy of this architecture".

And so he did (leaving his hosts little choice in the matter). Here are the details of this memorable meal.

Fried Eggs
Braised Capon
Valenciennes Rice
Cheeseboard
Basket of Apricots

Joachim Carvallo's Chicken à la Valencienne laid out in a Montereau dinner service.

ŒUFS FRITS

Fried Eggs

Poach the eggs in simmering
water to which has been
added a touch of vinegar.
Set aside on a white cloth.
Fry the bread in olive oil
with a touch of saffron
and a little vanilla. Heat the oil
in a deep-fat fryer and cook
the eggs in it until they are crisp.
Lay them on the fried bread
and garnish with thin slices
of cured but uncooked ham.

CHAPON BRAISÉ RIZ À LA VALENCIENNE

Braised Capon Valenciennes Rice

Take a good-sized capon or,
if not available, a plump
chicken. Slash all over
with a knife and push thin
slices of red pimentos and
whole, blanched almonds
into the slits.
Pour some olive oil over
the capon and cook
in a hot oven for 1 hour.
Meanwhile, prepare the
Valenciennes rice.
Cook the rice in boiling,
salted water until just cooked.
Slice some good red tomatoes,
thinly slice some peppers,
onions and aubergines.
Cook the ingredients separately
in olive oil and set aside
in a warm place.

To ensure that the vegetables
keep their colour,
do not overcook; they are never
better than when prepared
"al dente" i.e. crisp.
When the capon is cooked,
cut into pieces. Put the rice
on a serving dish and cover
with the various vegetables.
Serve with chopped herbs from
the garden, olives, pimentos
and olive oil pounded
with a pestle and mortar
(replace the olive oil with
cooking stock if preferred).

*Let us leave Guitte Carvallo
to have the final say*

"It was obvious that our hosts
knew nothing about Hispano-
Moorish cuisine. This dazzling
dish turned to fire as soon
as it reached the guests' palates
and throats. Faces immediately
flushed but conversation
flagged!"

An Easter Menu

A festive menu served in Villandry on Easter Sunday when guests enjoy the first asparagus from the greenhouses "accompanied by a frothy, buttercup-yellow sauce". Then comes the paschal lamb served on a silver platter. And strawberries in red Cabernet wine. If there are no strawberries, there are the traditional Easter chocolates.

ASPERGES
SAUCE MOUSSELINE

Asparagus Mousseline Sauce

Clean the asparagus well then place with tips uppermost in a cooking basket (if you do not have one, use a large tin with holes in the sides and base). Cook the asparagus in simmering water for approximately twenty minutes. Lay out on a serviette. Then prepare the Mousseline Sauce. It is, in fact, a hollandaise sauce to which is added some crème fraîche.

Sauce mousseline

On a very low heat, beat six egg yolks and a tablespoon of water per yolk until the mixture begins to froth. Ensure that it is not allowed to boil. Add 300 g clarified butter (i.e. the butter has melted slowly and the whey has dropped to the bottom). Stirring gently without allowing the mixture to boil, add one or two spoonfuls of preheated and stirred crème fraîche.

Keep the sauce warm in a bain-marie while you lay the well-drained asparagus out on the serving dish.

AGNEAU PASCAL
À LA MOSAÏQUE DE PRIMEURS DU JARDIN

Paschal Lamb with Early Spring Vegetables

Place a good leg of lamb in an ovenproof dish, cover with oil and dot with butter. Season with pepper. When the oven is hot, put the lamb in to cook, allowing 15 minutes per lb. Baste from time to time with the cooking stock. When the cooking time is finished, turn off the heat and leave the lamb in the oven for 10 minutes. Discard the cooking fat and pour on a generous glass of water then allow to reduce. Serve this "gravy" in a sauce boat. While the lamb is cooking, prepare all the vegetables from the garden[1] . Peel, chop or slice ensuring that all the vegetables are cut in the same way, and

cook in water. Drain and place in a large sauté pan with a good knob of butter. Cook until golden brown, over a low heat. Slice the lamb and lay on the serving dish surrounded by the vegetables.

LES FRAISES
AU VIN ROUGE

Strawberries in Red Wine

Wash the strawberries and remove the stems. Heat 1 litre good red wine with some cinnamon, one clove, and some blanched orange and lemon peel. Put the strawberries in the wine for 5 minutes, then remove and place in a fruit bowl. Bring the wine to the boil and leave to reduce slightly then filter and pour over the strawberries. Set aside in a cool place. Serve with mint leaves. The best wines for this dessert are a good Cabernet-Franc, a Chinon or a Bourgueil.

1. This means from a normal garden. Villandry has so many different vegetables that there has to be a choice.

VELOUTÉ DE POTIRON

Pumpkin Soup

Peel the pumpkin, remove the seeds and filaments. Dice and place in a pan, covered with milk. Sauté a chopped onion and the white part of a thinly-sliced leek, without allowing them to colour. Add the cooked pumpkin and the cooking milk. Mix in a blender or grind through a vegetable mill.

Add some more milk and some crème fraîche. Season with salt and pepper. If the soup is too thick, add some more milk or cream. Decorate with chervil. The pumpkin is coming back into its own, decorating gardens and producing mild-flavoured soups that are a blend of the sweet and the peppery. It has always been grown in the vegetable garden in Villandry. In this photo, it is being served in the Rochecotte Tureen, which has a history worth recounting. Rochecotte was once the residence of the Castellane family and Talleyrand was a frequent visitor to "the château of elegance and good taste". During a dinner, Madame Carvallo admired a Louis XV soup tureen made of Lunéville faïence and decorated with seasonal vegetables picked out in relief. The next morning, a chauffeur from Rochecotte arrived to give her the beautiful soup tureen accompanied by a card from the Marquise de Castellane bearing the words, "You took to me and I took to you". After being used for all the family's festive meals in Villandry and being taken to l'Escurial for some time, the Rochecotte Tureen has returned to present Pumpkin Soup from France's leading vegetable garden.

Among Villandry's very varied collections is this 18th-century bronze and copper ewer from northern India.
Below: Pumpkin Soup served in the Rochecotte soup tureen.

Villandry's famous vegetable garden is only one of the gardens recreated by Joachim Carvallo.
There is also a garden of simples, a flower garden laid out with square beds illustrating "Tragic Love", "Fickle Love", "Tender Love" and "Insane Love", another flower garden symbolising music, and a traditional water garden.
As to the vegetable garden, it inevitably varies depending on the season. In these autumnal photographs, it displays peppers, golden celery, blue leeks, purple sorrel, various ornamental cabbages, chard, totem tomatoes, cardoons... and, of course, pumpkins.

DEUX RECETTES DE FROMAGE DE LA GIRAUDIÈRE

Two Cheese Recipes from La Giraudière

Recipes from a neighbouring farm

Touraine produces numerous varieties of goat's cheeses which are served with local white Sauvignon wines. The first recipe is simple and delicious. Wrap a small goat's cheese ("Crottin de chèvre") in a thin slice of smoked bacon. Leave in a cool place for 3 days then brush with olive oil and heat in the oven.

Gâteau au fromage
Cheesecake

Take a sufficient quantity of flour to make an ordinary cake. Make a well in the middle and add a quantity of butter equal to two-thirds of the weight of flour. Then add sufficient water to make a reasonable dough. Add some salt and knead well.
Roll out and add a layer of soft but not skimmed cheese.
Fold into four, roll out again and fold up again.
Repeat this operation several times. Shape the cake, brush with milk and bake.

This is the silver baptismal place setting given to Anne Colleman, Joachim Carvallo's wife.
It now belongs to François, Henri and Angélique Carvallo's young son.

LES RÉAUX

The welcoming château

*T*he delightful dining room in the Château des Réaux was once the stables. As in many other châteaux, the owners' rooms were on the first floor. All that remains of the original castle is the tall gatehouse with its skilful brick and stone bonding topped by a square lookout post. This late 15th-century construction was commissioned by the Briçonnet family who also commissioned Chenonceau and Azay-le-Rideau. It was a great family (one of its descendants was none other than Sully) who led the way in the art of building during the Renaissance period. The systems of defence in châteaux were designed differently to suggest power and might while the interiors placed the emphasis on creature comforts and a good supply of natural light. This was then "Le Plessis-Rideau". Gédéon Tallemant des Réaux renamed it in 1653 and it has kept this new name ever since. After his death, Les Réaux was sold to the Taboureau family who kept it until 1895. The 18th-century pavilion beyond the gatehouse is known as the "Taboureau building"; it is an austere construction built of beautiful white stone. The château was purchased in 1895 by Julien Barois, Inspector General of Highways and Bridges, great-grandfather of Florence de Rendinger who now lives in the château with her husband, Jean-Luc de Goupil de Bouillé, a descendant of an old Touraine family. Julien Barois had a small pavilion built over the ruins of an older construction on the south side of the gatehouse, decorating it with the same checkerboard pattern. He included stained-glass windows which turned the interior into an oriental folly! The Loire supplies the water for the moat encircling the château and the small outbuildings.

The main drawing rooms on the upper floor are flooded with light. They are richly furnished and the paper on the walls in one of them has been listed as a historic monument. However, when Jean-Luc and Florence de Bouillé moved into Les Réaux in 1979, it had been unoccupied for fifteen years and everything remained to be done. The apartments had to be subdivided into smaller rooms, there was no running water, electricity or, of course, heating... Gradually, they refurbished the entire château, one room at a time and now each one is tastefully, often humorously, decorated. Having thought about their guests, they are now beginning on their private apartments which will be on the ground floor, because all the upper floors in Les Réaux are now back in use! This is a château which has aroused a great deal of enthusiasm and this sense of enjoyment seems to be communicative since their daughter, Angélique, Mme Carvallo, now runs the Château de Villandry, the other jewel in the crown of the Loire Valley.

Three silver eggcups. One of them is amusingly shaped like an egg on legs!

This set of 19th-century engravings can be seen in many different places. It provides an invaluable insight into the condition of the various châteaux. This view does not include the small Oriental-style pavilion built shortly afterwards, to the right of the gatehouse.

An attractive modern terrine perched on the wall above the moat in Les Réaux.

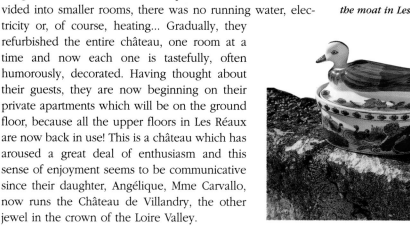

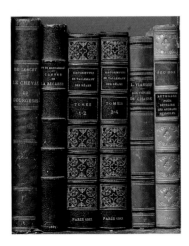

"Louis, by the grace of God, King of France and Navarre, to all present and future, we greet you. Our beloved Gédéon Tallemant, Lord of Les Réaux, has showed us that, since childhood, he has been known by the name of Les Réaux and that he has recently purchased the land and castellany of Le Plessis-Rideau, situated in the valley near the river Loire, which was sold to him with all its appurtenances and outbuildings and all manorial and other rights by François de La Béraudière, Marquis de l'Isle-Rouche and Lady Françoise de Machcoul, his spouse, for the sum of one hundred and fifteen thousand livres. The said land and castellany of Le Plessis-Rideau, being consequently in his family, he would like to change its name to Les Réaux, the name which he has always borne himself [...]. Let it be known that [...]. we have permitted and granted him [...] the right to change the name of the said land and castellany of Le Plessis-Rideau and that, in its place, this shall henceforth be known for all time as Les Réaux.
Signed: LOUIS, 1653. "

When signing these letters patent, Louis XIV did not know that Gédéon Tallemant des Réaux would, one day, be famous as the most irreverent chronicler of the century. It was not until 1834 that his *Historiettes* were published for the first time; they had been kept in his family since his death *c.* 1700. Born into the wealthy upper middle class, Tallemant des Réaux was no kinder to his own class than to the aristocracy. Since he wrote "only for himself and for a few friends", he emphasised the private, and often highly licentious, side of the life of the personalities of his day. Sometimes with a degree of bad faith! Overall, however, the work is a mine of information and we have made copious use of it.

The gatehouse, a mosaic of stone and brickwork decorated with the salamander of Francis I and the ermine of Anne of Brittany.

The recipes from the châteaux des RÉAUX

KOULIBIAC
DE SAUMON FUMÉ

Smoked Salmon Koulibiac

Breakfast is always carefully prepared at Les Réaux and is never a rushed meal.

Buy 200 g flaky pastry. Chop two onions and cook them in milk. Scramble five eggs, season with salt and pepper and add a little crème fraîche. Chop 200 g button mushrooms and fry lightly to brown. Cut 200 g smoked salmon into strips. Lay one-half of the pastry in a rectangular tin and fill with alternate layers of onion, egg, salmon and mushrooms. Cover with the remaining pastry. Make a little funnel and brush with egg yolk. Bake in a moderate oven until the pastry is golden brown.

SOUFFLÉ AU FROMAGE

Cheese Soufflé

Melt 75 g butter with 75 g Swiss cheese in a small saucepan. Mix in 75 g flour without allowing to cook then pour on 50 cl boiling milk. Mix well, season with salt and pepper and add a touch of nutmeg. Allow the mixture to cool then add six egg yolks and a little crème fraîche. Beat the egg whites with a pinch of salt until very stiff and fold into the mixture. Pour into a greased and floured soufflé mould and cook in a moderate oven (approximately 180 ° C) for 15 minutes.

SANDRE
AU BEURRE ROUGE

Pike Perch
in Red Butter

Prepare a well-seasoned fish
stock: in a fish kettle
one-third filled with water,
add two-thirds dry white wine,
three slices of lemon, one
roughly chopped onion,
one sliced carrot, peppercorns,
coarse salt, thyme, bay,
and some parsley stalks.
Bring to the boil, cover
and simmer on a low heat
for 30 minutes.
Meanwhile, wash the pike-perch
fillets. Divide into as many
portions as there are guests.
Chop two shallots
(preferably grey shallots)
and reduce in red Bourgueil
wine. Remove from the heat to
ensure that some liquid remains.
Set aside.
Lay the pike-perch fillets in the
stock. Turn off the heat and
keep the pan covered.
Remove the butter from
the fridge, cut into small cubes,
place the reduction back
on the heat and season with salt
and pepper. Gradually add
the butter, beating hard.
You can also add a spoonful
of crème fraîche to ensure that
the red butter remains light
while you prepare the fish.
Put the pike-perch fillets on
absorbent kitchen paper
then lay them on hot plates
and pour the sauce
over the top.
Serve with boiled potatoes.

MAGRET DE CANARD
AUX POMMES

Duck Breasts
with Apples

*Florence de Bouillé serves her
duck breasts with a good
Bourgueil from the nearby
vineyard.*

With this dish, you can serve
several sorts of steamed
vegetables: string beans, carrots
and turnips browned on all sides
or small sautéed potatoes.
Peel a few apples, cut into
quarters and sprinkle with lemon
juice. Set aside while you cook
the duck. Place some goose fat
in a large frying pan to melt.
When the fat is very hot, lay the
duck breasts in the pan skin side
downwards, and fry quickly to
seal in the juices. Then turn the
heat down and turn the breasts
over. Cook for approximately
ten minutes (the meat should
be pink). Remove the duck
and keep warm. Discard the
cooking fat and pour in some
water or white wine.
Reduce by boiling hard.
Melt some butter in a small
frying pan and fry the apple
pieces over a low heat until
golden on all sides.
When the sauce has reduced,
add a generous knob of butter,
remove the pan from the heat
and allow the butter to melt.
Cut the duck breasts into thin
slices and lay them out on plates
or on a serving dish.
Pour over the sauce, garnish
with the golden apples
and the selection
of small vegetables.

FEUILLETÉ AUX POIRES

Pear Pastry

Cut a circle of flaky pastry
to the size you want.
Lay the pastry on a buttered
baking tray.
Finely chop a few pears
cooked in a light syrup.
Lay the pear slices
on the pastry so that
they look attractive.
Place in a hot oven until
the pastry is golden brown
and crisp.

VACHERIN SANS GLACE DE DANY

Dany's Meringue Dessert

Mix four egg yolks with four
spoonfuls of crème fraîche and
four spoonfuls of sugar and beat
until smooth. Beat the egg whites
until firm and fold into the mixture. Pour one-half of the mixture into a mould, lay on some
crushed meringues then pour on
the remainder of the mixture. Put
in the deep freeze for 24 hours
and serve with a raspberry sauce.

GÂTEAU AU CHOCOLAT DES RÉAUX

Les Réaux Chocolate Swiss Roll

Cover a baking tray
with buttered aluminium foil
sprinkled with flour.
Separate nine eggs.
Add half-a-teacup of sugar
to the yolks and heat
over a pan of hot water.
Mix with a beater until white
and thick.
Melt 200 g chocolate
in a bain-marie and add
to the mixture with
a tablespoonful of flour.
Beat the egg whites
with two tbsp. of sugar until
stiff. Carefully fold into
the chocolate mixture.
Pour into the baking tray
and bake for 10 minutes
at 150 ° C.
When the cake is cooked,
turn it out onto a teatowel.
Spread with strawberry jam
and cream whipped up with a
little raspberry syrup
(or chocolate mousse
if preferred).
Carefully roll up and decorate
with icing sugar,
strawberries,
and strawberry sauce.

FESSES DE BONNE SŒUR

Nun's Rump

This dessert requires some concentration. It has to be made without interruptions and without trying to do anything else at the same time. You will need approximately half-an-hour of absolute peace and quiet. Beat six egg whites with 25 g sugar until very stiff. In a saucepan, caramelise 150 g sugar very slowly, **without water**. When the caramel is pale golden, fold very quickly but very carefully into the beaten egg whites. Pour the mixture into a mould greased with almond oil and place in the freezer for 12 hours. Then remove from the mould and enjoy this cheeky little dessert!

PELOTES DE SORBETS

Water Ices

This is an easy, unusual dessert that always makes an impression. Buy or make black-currant sorbet, tangerine sorbet, and pear or lemon sorbet. Wash some green and black grapes and some strawberries. Crush some meringues (the quantity depends on the size of the serving dish). Cover the dish with crushed meringues then build up a pyramid of scoops of water ices, alternating the colours. Once the pyramid is complete, decorate with grapes and strawberries placed between the scoops. Carefully put back into the deep freeze. Serve with a fruit sauce served in a sauceboat.

The Château des Réaux rising up in the early morning mist from the nearby River Loire.

USSÉ

The Sleeping Beauty's castle

A wonderful coffee in the king's bedchamber. Above, left, the crest of the Blacas family: "d'argent a la comete with sixteen rais de gueule". The Blacas are an old provençal family said by Nostradamus to have come from Aragon. The comet on their coat-of-arms is a reference to one of the Magi who is traditionally said in the family to be one of their ancestors. Several Blacas family members were allies of the sovereign counts of Toulon in the 12th century; another was a famous troubadour in the 13th cenury. The first Duc de Blacas offered, in vain, to give up his own freedom in exchange for the king's liberation during the French Revolution. Since 1821, the family has held the title of duke and peer.

The King's Bedchamber in the Château d'Ussé was originally designed for Louis XIV but he never visited the château. It was refurbished in 1770 and hung with silk from Tours which can still be seen in the bed-hangings. Eventually, it was the King of Kings, Haile Selassie, Emperor of Ethiopia, who took a nap here during a visit to Ussé, opposite the portrait of Mlle de Blois, Louis XIV's daughter. The Château d'Ussé was frequently altered but the white tuff, a stone which is so wonderful for sculptures, has ensured that it retains its unity. There is known to have been a Lord of Ussé around the year 1,000. He was a Dane named Gueldin I who defeated the fearsome Fulk Nerra, Count of Anjou, on more than one occasion, a rare feat indeed. The construction of the château, however, is

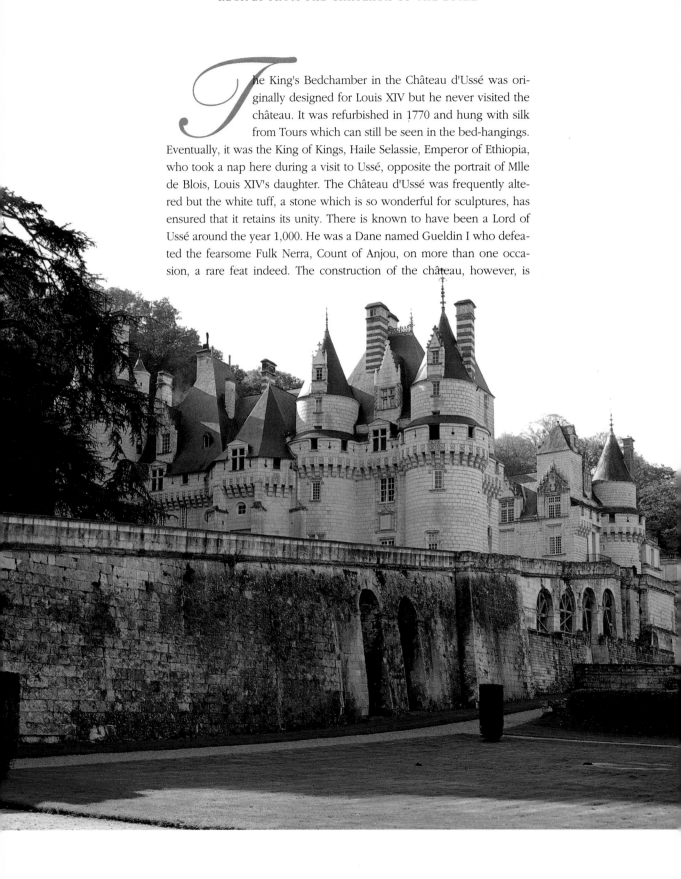

attributed to Jean de Bueil who sold it in 1485 to Jacques d'Espinay, a nobleman from Brittany. The family kept it until 1557, increasing and extending it. Ussé was then shaped like a closed quadrilateral topped by a large keep. After several sales, it became the property of the Valentinay family, one of whose sons married Vauban's daughter. The numerous buildings designed by Vauban throughout France are well-known; in this instance, he was credited with alterations that he did not do. The building on the north side was probably demolished before his time in order to give an unrestricted view of the newly-built terraces. In 1780, the château was again sold and, in 1807, it was purchased by the Duc de Duras. It has been passed down through the family to the Blacas who live in it today. Casimir, Marquis de Blacas, is a great connoisseur of good red and white wines from the Loire Valley. And it is true that the area which produces Chinon lies adjacent to the hillsides of Rigny-Ussé.

*The private dining room
in the château.*

VELOUTÉ DE CHAMPIGNONS D'USSÉ

Ussé Mushroom Soup

Clean 400 g button mushrooms and slice lengthways. Melt 30 g butter and fry the mushrooms. Add 30 g flour and stir. Pour on 40 cl hot milk and 40 cl chicken stock. Mix and cook for 20 minutes. Mix in a blender, season with salt and pepper, and add a little crème fraîche before serving.

SOUFFLÉ À LA VANILLE DE JACQUELINE

Jacqueline's Vanilla Soufflé

Heat 40 cl milk with a split vanilla pod and 100 g sugar. Make a roux with 100 g butter and 50 g flour. Remove from the heat and add five egg yolks. Mix well and set aside. Beat the egg whites with a pinch of salt until stiff. Fold the whites into the mixture and cook in a hot oven for approximately 20 minutes. When the soufflé has risen, serve immediately. Remember "Guests can wait for a soufflé but a soufflé cannot wait for the guests".

CANARD AUX OLIVES

Casimir de Blacas is a great huntsman and game is often served at Ussé.

After plucking and drawing a duck, cook in boiling stock (e.g. beef stock) for 20 minutes on a low heat. Remove the duck, drain and dry. Melt some goose fat or olive oil in an oval pan. When hot, place the duck in it and turn frequently to brown on all sides. Lower the heat, cover and cook for 30 minutes (you may need less time for smaller ducks). Meanwhile, stone some green and black olives and macerate in the stock. Ten minutes before serving, drain the olives and place in the pan with the duck. By cooking the duck twice, it remains tender.

Left: In the former chapel turned into a Louis XIV drawing room, there is an anonymous painting of a sultan's feast. The large pieces of meat roasting over the fire, however, are timeless. Below: A close-up of the "Wedding Feast in Canaan", a copy of a painting by Veronese which hangs in the Louvre.

GIGUE DE CHEVREUIL SAUCE JACQUELINE

Haunch of Venison with Jacqueline's Own Sauce

Prepare a marinade for the venison the day before it is to be served. Use a red wine with good body, plenty of spices, thyme, bay, and coarse-ground pepper. Turn the haunch over from time to time to ensure that it is well-marinated. Preheat the oven. Wrap the haunch in thin slices of pork fat (Jacqueline cooks a piece of beef on the previous day then keeps the same pork fat to wrap round the venison). Add some butter and the juice from the meat. Leave for 1 1/2 hours. Prepare the sauce by making a roux.

Sieve the marinade and pour into the roux. Mix well and, like Jacqueline, add the "juice" from the previous day's roast beef. Cook over a low heat. When the venison is cooked, leave it at the door of the oven for 10 minutes. This makes it even more tender. Remove the pork fat, slice the venison, lay on a serving dish and pour the sauce over the meat. Jacqueline garnishes this dish with mashed celeriac and cranberries.

LES POIRES TAPÉES DE RIVARENNES

Tapped Rivarennes Pears

Not far from Rigny-Ussé is the village of Rivarennes which is famous for its "tapped pears" prepared in cave dwellings in the tuff cliffs. The pears are peeled but not cored, then dried for 4 days in a bread oven so that they lose 70% of their volume. They are then "tapped" to remove the remaining air and can be stored dry or in jars. To use them, "re-inflate" them before cooking, preferably by soaking in Chinon wine. They are delicious served with meat in sauce or game dishes.

BISCUITS À LA CUILLÈRE

Sponge Fingers

Beat 250 g castor sugar in a bowl with eight egg yolks until thick enough to coat the spoon. Add flavouring (lemon juice, orange flower water, vanilla essence etc.). Add 200 g dry sieved flour. Beat the eight egg whites until very stiff and fold them into the mixture.
Put in an icing bag wide enough to form fingers. Force out the mixture onto greaseproof paper 10 cm long and sprinkle with castor sugar (remember to dust off the excess sugar).
When the sugar has melted, place the biscuits in a very low oven and leave the door open for a few minutes.
Then close the oven door and bake the biscuits for approximately 20 minutes.
When they are golden, remove from the oven, prise them away from the greaseproof paper and store in a dry place.

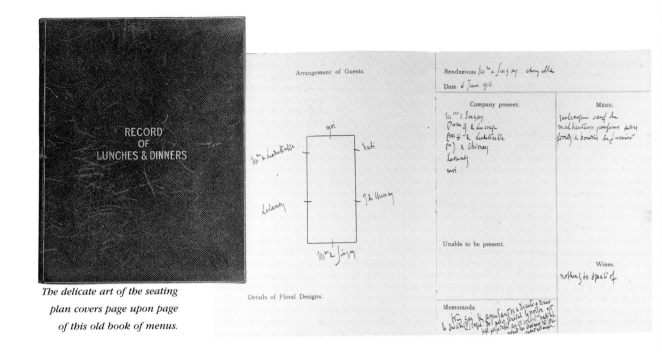

Arrangement of Guests.

Rendezvous *Mme de Sugay chapelle*

Date 6 Juin 1910

Details of Floral Designs.

Company present.

Mme de Sugay
Pierre de duc cinqe
Cte # de duclaverille
Pce J. de Chimay
Laurenty
moi

MENU.

Unable to be present.

Wines.

Memoranda

The delicate art of the seating plan covers page upon page of this old book of menus.

The hill on which the Château d'Ussé is built contains deep cellars which are said to run to Saint-Benoît-la-Forêt 4 kms - 2 1/2 miles away by an underground passage. It is known that, in 1560, René d'Espinay planted Pineau de la Loire grapes on the hillside, a stock now better-known as Chenin. From this vineyard on the plateau, a chute dug into the tuff enables the grapes to be poured directly down into the wine press. Casimir de Blacas' cellars contain some old bottles that have remained unmarked by age - dry or sweet Chenins, purple Chinons, and even a few old Grolleaux, the successful result of a variety that has been too heavily criticised.

Montreuil Bellay

Bellay

A gem preserved for all time

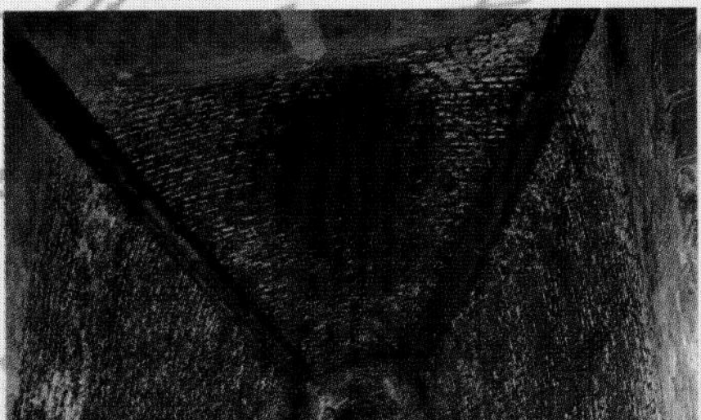

The soot that covers
the sides of this central
fireplace dates from
before the Renaissance.

*T*he vines that blaze in the fireplace in the Château de Montreuil-Bellay are one hundred years old or more. After producing their share of good brilliantly-coloured Saumur with a bouquet redolent of red fruit, they have been pulled up to leave way for young vines. The kitchen, on the other hand, has not changed in five hundred years and it is easy to see at a glance how cooking methods have developed since the 14th century. First, there was a central hearth, a tall pyramid with a hole in it. Entire carcasses were cooked in the centre of the room. In order to ensure that the air circulated correctly and that the enormous cooking hood had an air supply, two ducts were built in the 15th century and, later, turned into real fireplaces. Those were the days of pot-hooks and cooking pots. A bread oven was then added on to the side of one of the fireplaces. The furnishings and fittings were perfected over the following centuries. There was a stove on which food could be simmered slowly over the embers and finally, the latest available mod. con. in the 19th century, a vast cast-iron multi-oven stove. Nothing much new has been invented since then!

This kitchen is unusual for its size, for the monumental ribbed vaulting and, more particularly, for its location at the corner of the inner courtyard, oppos-ite the "New Castle". It stands at some distance from the château to decrease the fire risk. A gallery which has since been demolished used to link the two buildings.

The earliest construction of a castle was attributed to Fulk Nerra, the great builder of the year 1,000 A.D. The keep was then given to the Berlay, or Bellay, family, local noblemen who no doubt gave their name to the town. They were subjects of the King of France and the Count of Anjou, a situation which became untenable when the Plantagenet Count of Anjou became King of England. After a siege lasting almost one year, the building was destroyed by Geoffrey Plantagenet in 1151. A new fortress was erected one hundred years later, as were the town walls that can still be seen today. Montreuil-Bellay was handed down through successive generations until, in 1415, it became the property of the d'Harcourts who commissioned further building (château, collegiate church, tithe barn etc.). Later owners of the château included the Orléans-Longueville family, the Maréchal de la Meilleraye, the Cossé-Brissac family, and the La Trémoille family which sold the château in 1822. Since then, it has been passed on by marriage and is now owned by Chantal de Grandmaison who lives there with her husband, Xavier de Thuy.

The various constructions were erected on a spur of rock overlooking the R. Thouet. The earliest building was the 13th-century gatehouse through which assailants were forced to pass. There, they could be fired on from the barbican. Beyond is the barbican, followed by the old castle of the d'Harcourts, the canons' residences, and four small houses each with a staircase designed for the priests of the collegiate church. Finally, there is the Château Neuf, the "new castle" on which building began in 1485. A pupil of Viollet-le-Duc completed the entrance to this château in 1860. It includes a remarkable spiral staircase and a few treasures such as the marriage chest of Henry IV and his wife, Margot. All the buildings huddle close together on the narrow promontory and all are isolated from the town by a dry moat. Montreuil-Bellay was

The gatehouse seen from outside the château. It is reached by two bridges set out of line with each other. This constituted a potential threat for attackers.

reputed to be an impregnable fortress, with natural defences, fortifications, an underground passage and deep cellars. It was here, in 1904, that the *Confrérie bachique des Sacavins* was founded, the oldest wine brotherhood in existence and an idea first mooted by Georges de Grandmaison. This was hardly surprising - it is a family that enjoys good food, as we shall see.

Monsieur de GRANDMAISON'S recipe books

Madame de Thuy's great-grandfather, Monsieur de Grandmaison, travelled extensively throughout the world after becoming a widower. When he was no longer able to travel, he began writing cookery books, all in long hand and all illustrated with original pen-and-ink drawings. Madame de Thuy lent us these extraordinary books and we have included a few extracts. We have, of course, left untouched the lively, poetic style. Monsieur de Grandmaison died in 1914.

TOURTEAU À LA GRANDMAISON

Grandmaison-style Crab

Choose a crab that is heavy
for its size and not frothy.
Cook in cold water with a handful of salt. Leave to cool.
For a large crab, finely chop
a raw onion then add a soupçon
of garlic and a shallot.
Chop some parsley,
tarragon and chervil and,
separately, two hard-boiled eggs,
putting the whites on one side
and the yolks on the other.
Open the crab, taking care to
keep the interior.
Keep the shell. Carefully extract
all the meat inside, discarding all
the cartilage. Break open the
claws and remove the meat.
Put the creamy interior
and the crab meat in a mortar
and pound, gradually adding
some olive oil, salt, white
pepper, a soupçon of cayenne
pepper, mixed spice,
raz el-hanoun, the onion,
garlic and shallot.
Pound to a paste.
Then add a drop of vinegar
or (preferably) a little lemon
juice. Fill the shell
with this mixture and decorate
the opening like a garden
with the chopped eggs and
herbs. Lay the shell
on the crab pincers for support.
Serve.

Crab à la Grandmaison.

SOUPE AU CONGRE

Eel Soup

Eel soup! I can imagine
your face when you read the
mere name of this dish!
That's disgusting... etc.
You are wrong. Ask my yachts-
men friends who, having tasted
it, all asked me for the recipe
which I am noting
in this book today.
Skin a black conger eel
(the type of eel is important),
preferably freshly caught.
Take masses of all sorts
of herbs, lettuce, watercress,
carrots, onions (not too many).
Prepare a bouquet garni
of parsley, thyme and bay.
You will also need three
or four marigold flowers.
In a pan, melt a knob
of butter the size of an egg
and brown the eel cut into
pieces for 2 minutes.
Add the chopped vegetables,
pour in 2 litres water, season
with salt and pepper.
Add the bouquet garni,
a pimento, and a shallot,
all of which should be removed
before serving. Cook over
a high heat for 20 minutes then
lower the heat and cook
for a further 1 hour. Serve.
N.B. The eel, which is removed
from the soup before serving,
should not be discarded. Eaten
cold the next day with oil and
vinegar, it deserves more than a
passing mention.

Brochet à la Rouland

Rouland-style Pike

My friend, Rouland, an old gamekeeper who has been employed by my family for nigh on thirty years, said to me one day, "When I was a young water bailiff, I used to cook fish for the gentlemen of the Highways and Bridges Department and it was finger-lickin' good. Sir, I shall give you the recipe and you can let me know whether it really is that delicious."
Sharing a bottle of chilled wine, I wrote the following to his dictation: Cut the fish into pieces and fry as if it were to be eaten like that. Then put the fish in a pan with a knob of butter as large as a hen's egg per 1 kg fish (proportionately increase the quantity of butter if there is more than 1 kg). Place on a low heat.

Sauce

Beat an egg with a spoonful of flour and half-a-spoonful of cornflour. Continue to beat while adding the equivalent of approximately one bowl of warm water (increase the quantities if there is more fish). Just before pouring the sauce into the pan in which the fish is simmering, add a drop of vinegar, beating all the time. Pour onto the fish and wait until the sauce thickens, over a low heat.
When the sauce has the required creamy consistency, add parsley, chervil, and finely chopped green onions just before serving hot.

Beans.

N.B. Sometimes in Anjou, very large fish are served with this sauce. I advise against it as the fish is not sufficiently fried. Do not use a pike-perch of more than 2 or 3 lbs. As to tench, perch and trout, they can always be used because they rarely exceed 1 kg in weight.
Should I tell you the truth? He was right. I tasted this dish and I did, indeed, lick my fingers clean.

Œufs à la coque truffés

Boiled Egg with Truffles

Take some freshly-laid eggs. Place them in a tin with a tight lid with a good-sized, peeled truffle or some truffle parings. Leave the eggs in the tin for 24 hours then remove them and boil them.

Serve with grilled, buttered fingers of bread. The eggs will be filled with the taste of truffles.

Le haricot

The Humble Bean

The world was created by the Master of All Things. Plants grew out of nothingness and to each He gave a purpose. Alone in its corner, the bean, an uncouth yokel of a plant, was making a terrible commotion. It had been forgotten. After hours of hard work, the Lord was taking a little nap but He was constantly woken up by sighs from the plant. "Who is this impertinent fellow?" He asked. The Archangel Gabriel, who was on duty that day, went away to enquire and immediately returned to tell the Lord what the bean was up to.

Having summoned the bean to appear before Him, the Eternal said, "You are an impertinent fellow. You doubted in me, yet you know that I have a purpose for everything. I knew you were a turbulent child and because of this, I intended to keep you in Paradise and ask you to blow the trumpet of the Day of Judgement. However, you have doubted me so go down to Earth and be good until all the centuries have passed." Such were the Lord's words and this was what happened. Since then, the bean has been grown worldwide. It is the gypsy of the stomach, always showing off and always noisy. It is, and will remain, the joy of some and the terror of others. Despite all its faults, it is delicious and it therefore has its rightful place here, not so that I can explain how to eat it with Fat Sauce, Thin Sauce, onions, as a garnish for a leg of lamb, as a salad vegetable etc. No, I should like to tell you how it is eaten, with great gusto, in the distant lands of South America, the land of groaning volcanoes. Take 2 lbs. dried beef or mutton and leave to soak overnight to remove the salt. Place the meat in boiling water for approximately 15 minutes then cut into strips. Soak an adequate quantity of beans for 24 hours. Put the vegetables in cold water and bring up to the boil. After 15 minutes, empty out the water and replace it with warm water. Then add the dried meat, two pig's ears, one pig's trotter, 1 lb. salt pork, onions, garlic, pepper, salt, bay and a pimento. Cover and bring to the boil until the beans become soft enough to crush between the fingers. Add a spoonful of oil or butter, cook for a further 10 minutes and serve.

Queue de bœuf en hochepot

Oxtail Hotpot

Cut the oxtail into pieces and blanch. Then cook in some good stock with a bouquet garni and very little salt. It takes 5 hours to cook the oxtail.

Halfway through the cooking time, add onions, carrots, parsnips, turnips and a little cabbage, all neatly chopped and blanched. When everything is cooked, put the meat on a cloth and wipe well to remove all traces of fat. Arrange the vegetables and meat in a clean earthenware pot that can be brought to the table. Degrease the sauce in which the meat has cooked. Add a little tomato puree and reduce if the sauce is too liquid. Take care not to add too much salt. Sieve the sauce and pour over the meat and vegetables to serve.

Oxtail Hotpot.

CHATEAUBRIAND
EN TERRINE
Chateaubriand Steak in a Terrine

Take an unpared piece
of fillet of beef weighing 500 -
600 g. Remove some of the fat.
Place it on the table and beat
so that it has the same thickness
on all sides. Place in a pan a
knob of butter the size
of a walnut and, when hot,
fry the steak, turning it over to
seal on all sides. This should be
done fairly quickly over a high
heat so that the meat does not
cook. Remove the fillet and
place on a plate, seasoning well
with salt and pepper.
Set to one side. Peel two spring
onions, three or four small carrots which should then be thinly
sliced, and four good-sized, firm,
ripe tomatoes soaked in boiling
water for a second so that they

can be skinned. Cut the
tomatoes in half and press them
slightly to remove the water
and pips (in winter, replace the
tomatoes by two large spoonfuls
of tomato puree).
Finely chop a small shallot.
Take a paté dish and place
one-half of the chopped
vegetables in the bottom.
Lay the steak over the top then
cover with the remainder
of the carrots and onions, pieces
of tomato cut into four, shallot,
a small bay leaf and a small
sprig of thyme. Pour a glass
of dry white Bordeaux over the
top, followed by a liqueur glass
of brandy, the same amount of
madeira and a small teaspoonful
of veal stock or other
very good stock.
Cover and seal with
flour-and-water paste.
Bake in a moderate oven for
2 hours. Present the paté dish
at the table as it is, without
removing the lid.
The wonderful smell is
mouthwatering before
the meal is even served and
Chateaubriand will be fidgeting
in his grave on the Island
of Grand Bé.

*Montreuil-Bellay
has its own vineyard
producing
red or rosé Saumurs.*

*A pot-hanger, copper
pots, and braziers
on the kitchen walls.
Below: A view of
the Château Neuf
from the courtyard.*

LE *L*UDE

A chef's dream

Left: Courgette Loaf.
And some produce
from the vegetable garden.
Above: "This article was shaped like
a frosted glass bowl with a goblet
of similar nature inside,
containing water mixed with mint".
Christian de Nicolaÿ mentioned

these strange, almost flower-shaped
objects, in his Memoirs.
In fact, although art has turned
them into things of beauty,
they had a hygienic purpose,
having been made as finger bowls.
These bear the coat-of-arms
of the Bourbons.

The vegetable garden at the Château du Lude is the pride and joy of Barbara de Nicolaÿ. It is both decorative and useful and it supplies an abundance of all sorts of fruit and vegetables, including cardoons and countless varieties of pumpkins and marrows which finish ripening in the great kitchen in the basement. This is a real castle kitchen and it is easy to imagine a large staff bustling round the back-draught stove. Nowadays, cooking is done in a different room in Le Lude. The kitchen is more modest but the food is still beautifully prepared. The Comte and Comtesse Louis-Jean de Nicolaÿ welcomed us to their home and showed us their family recipe books.

Set well to the north of the river, Le Lude is nevertheless one of the Loire Valley châteaux by its architecture. The first castle was designed in the 13th century; it consisted of a huge fortress with six towers well defended by a dry moat. It was nevertheless captured by the English

in 1425. Thirty years later, Jehan de Daillon, who came from an old aristocratic family in the Poitiers region, purchased the château. His family retained Le Lude for two hundred years, updating it to take account of Renaissance taste. The south wall still had two large towers but it was decorated with openings and medallions representing famous people, a string-course emphasising the division into storeys and wide mullioned windows. The château had abandoned its mediaeval defences, retaining only a few symbolic attributes.

When, in 1685, Henri de Daillon died without an heir, the Château du Lude passed to the Duc de Roquelaure then to the Rohan family who sold it in 1751. Upkeep had been scant and it was in a poor state of repair when it was purchased by a Frenchman of Dutch origin, Monsieur du Velaer, who renovated it and bequeathed it to his niece, Françoise Butler, Marquise de La Vieuville. Le Lude then passed to her daughter, Marquise de Talhouët, then to General Frédéric de Talhouët, then to Auguste, then to René, Marquis de Talhouët-Roy, Mayor of Le Lude for fifty-six years, then to his grandson, René de Nicolaÿ, father of Comte Louis-Jean de Nicolaÿ, the present owner. Each generation has made a contribution to the embellishment or conservation of the building. The house, with a courtyard that seems to belong to a Parisian mansion, one wall to the Touraine area, and the other to a Classical château, has digested all these additions without any problem. Proof, if ever there was, of a healthy appetite!

In this huge 15th-century chamber opening onto the empty moat, the kitchen still has its 19th-century layout. It is light, attractive and functional, indeed it is a chef's dream.

Left: The main dining room is decorated with 17th-century Flemish tapestries which were discovered beneath the parquet flooring where they had been hidden during the French Revolution. The design of the fireplace was inspired by the one in Blois and it includes the emblems of Francis I and Claude of France.

Recipes from Le *L*UDE

To accompany these recipes, we have borrowed a few lines from the memoirs entitled *Aux jours d'autrefois* by Christian de Nicolaÿ, Comte Louis-Jean's uncle.

Vegetable Garden Menu

Cardoons with Marrowbone

Loir Perch à la Meunière

Red Fruit Pavlova

Photo below:

"Christmas lunch was a protracted affair because of the abundance of dishes, which were listed on a silver-framed menu handed round the table".

Cardoons with Marrowbone.

CARDONS À LA MOELLE
Cardoons with Marrowbones

Select cardoons with very white stems. Peel the stems and rub them with lemon to prevent discoloration. Cut into pieces approximately 10 cm (4 inches) in length. Cook in a pan of lightly-boiling salted water with a few slices of lemon to ensure that the cardoons remain white. Keep a watchful eye on the cooking - it can require 10 minutes or 1 1/2 hours depending on the ripeness of the cardoons and this, in turn, depends on how much sun they have had in summer and whether or not there has been an early frost. Cardoons are reputed to be tender only if they have been subjected to the first frosts of the winter. When cooked, they should be tender but crisp. Prepare a roux, adding meat extract for flavour. Fry some croûtons in a little butter. Finely chop some ham and hard-boiled eggs. Cook the marrowbones in boiling water. Remove the bone marrow at the last moment and place on the croûtons. Mix the cardoons into the sauce, lay out on a serving dish and garnish with the croûtons topped with chopped ham, hard-boiled eggs and bone marrow. Serve immediately.

PERCHE DU LOIR MEUNIÈRE
Loir Perch à La Meunière

To prepare perch *à la meunière,* the fish should be neither too big nor too small (small fish are prepared differently). So, take a medium-sized perch, snip off the fins, scale it and rinse. After drying it, roll in flour. Hold it by the tail and tap to ensure that the coating of flour does not contain lumps. Melt a small quantity of oil and a knob of butter. When very hot, lay the perch in the pan, still over a strong heat. Cook for 5 minutes. Lower the heat and turn the fish onto the other side. Leave to cook for 10 minutes while you prepare the lemons.

Wash and dry them. Using a fluting utensil, remove regular strips of lemon peel, working from the top of the lemon to the base. Make eight regularly-spaced grooves. Then slice the lemons thinly and set aside. Press one lemon and retain the juice. When the perch is cooked, season with salt and pepper. Place it on a silver platter. Discard the cooking fat and replace with a generous knob of butter which should be melted and allowed to cook until it is golden brown. Add the lemon juice. Pour over the perch, decorate with fine strips of lemon peel and some parsley. Perch served in this manner should be garnished with boiled potatoes. "The fish arrived with the tide, or were fished directly from the river. Loir perch was justifiably famous."

Loir perch à la meunière

Meringue
Aux Fruits Rouges
Red Fruit Pavlova

4 egg whites
150 g castor sugar
vanilla essence
seasonal fruit: raspberries,
strawberries, redcurrants etc.
25 g crème fraîche

This double sauce-boat bearing the crest of the Talhouët-Roy family is designed to keep the sauce hot.

Beat the egg white with an electric beater for 15 minutes, adding the sugar in three stages, approximately every 5 minutes. Add 1 tsp. vanilla essence and continue to beat as long as possible until very stiff. Butter a sheet of greaseproof paper and line a circular pie dish. Using a wooden spoon, spread the egg whites over the dish, ensuring that they form a layer approximately 2 cm (3/4 inch) thick. Bake in a very low oven (60-80 °C) for a few hours. Check from time to time and remove the meringue when the outside is hard but not crumbly. The oven can be turned off and the meringue can be left inside until the oven is completely cold, if preferred. Cover the meringue with a layer of lightly-sweetened whipped cream and garnish with red fruit.

"So great was the influence of my grandmother (Marguerite de Talhouët-Roy) on successive cooks, Théophile or Laliot or Maret, that the food always had the same characteristics as if the same hand had presided over its preparation, year in, year out."

PAIN DE COURGETTES
Courgette Loaf

Slice three yellow courgettes
(they hold their texture well)
and three green courgettes
(they add colour) without
peeling. Fry with a few
spoonfuls of olive oil, then add
a little water and cook over
a moderate heat. Reduce well.
When all the water has
evaporated, remove the
courgettes from the heat and
puree in a blender.
Beat four eggs with a glassful
of crème fraîche and some
sprigs of basil (or tarragon)
and add to the pureed
courgettes. Season with salt
and pepper. If the puree is too
liquid, add a few sheets
of gelatine dissolved in water.
Butter a ring mould or loaf tin.
Pour in the mixture and bake in
a bain-marie in the oven for
45 minutes, using a moderate
setting. Meanwhile, prepare
a tomato sauce. Blanch 500 g
tomatoes so that they are easier
to peel. Fry a clove of garlic and
one chopped onion until golden
brown in three tablespoonfuls

olive oil. Remove the garlic
and add the tomatoes cut into
pieces and a few bay leaves.
Leave to cook over a moderate
heat, stirring occasionally.
Sieve the tomatoes or mix
in a blender. Return to the heat
and leave to reduce.
If necessary, add some tomato
puree to add flavour and
thicken. Remove the courgette
loaf from the tin, place
on a serving dish and
pour on the tomato sauce.
Serve hot or cold.

RAVIOLIS À LA CRÈME
Ravioli in Cream Sauce

400 g flour
2 eggs and a little water
Filling:
400 g fresh goat's cheese
400 g buffalo-milk mozzarella
a bunch of parsley
salt and pepper

Make a well in the middle
of the flour. Pour in the beaten
eggs and add a little salt.
Mix and knead with the
fingertips, adding a little water
if the dough is too stiff.
Work the dough by spreading
it out and folding it back up
occasionally until it is firm and
pliable (15 minutes or more).
Leave the dough to rest for
1 hour. Meanwhile, prepare
the filling. Cut the mozzarella
into small cubes (buffalo-milk
cheese is much tastier than
the cow's milk equivalent).
Break up the goat's cheese
with a fork, chop the parsley
in an electric herb mill,

and mix all the ingredients
with a little salt and a generous
quantity of pepper until
well-blended and smooth.
Roll out the dough as thinly
as possible. If you do not have
a ravioli mould, work on only
one-half of the dough, dotting
small heaps of filling
approximately every 4 cm
(1 1/2 inches) apart. Fold the
other half of the dough over
the top, press the edges together
and cut out small, regular-sized
"cushions" using an indented
wheel-type pastry-cutter.
Put the ravioli into boiling,
salted water for a few minutes,
then dry and mix with cream
flavoured with pepper and
parsley. Serve with grated
parmesan.
Variation: Instead of cooking
the ravioli in boiling water,
cook it in a deep fat fryer and
serve without the cream sauce.
Cooked this way, it is called
Panzarotti!

ŒUFS BRAYONS
Brayon Eggs

4 eggs, 20 cl cream,
milk, salt, pepper, fines herbes,
tomato sauce

Beat all the ingredients together
as if making an omelette.
Butter a ring mould and fill
two-thirds full with the egg
mixture. Bake in a bain-marie
in the oven for 30 minutes.
Turn out onto a round
serving dish and pour over
tomato sauce or a tomato-
flavoured bechamel sauce.

MONT-BLANC
Mont-Blanc Dessert

500 g chestnuts
dark chocolate, one glass milk,
sugar, whipped cream,
vanilla essence

Cook the chestnuts
in the milk, sugar and 1 tsp.
vanilla essence for 20 minutes,
stirring occasionally.
After peeling the chestnuts,
break them up with a fork
and add a bar of chocolate
broken into pieces.
Replace over the heat and stir
occasionally until the chocolate
has melted.
Mix in a food blender.
Return to the heat and stir until
the "puree" is smooth.
If it is too stiff, add some milk.
Leave to cool. Take a round
dish. Puree the mixture
a second time and heap up
on the serving dish, sprinkling
with vermicelli.
Make a well in the centre
and fill with whipped cream.
Decorate as the mood
takes you then chill the dessert
in the fridge for a few hours.
Serve when very cold.

CHOU ROUGE À LA FLAMANDE
Flemish-style Red Cabbage

For one cabbage,
take four apples, one onion,
some sugar and vinegar.
Thinly slice the cabbage.
Chop the onion and fry
in a little butter until golden
brown then add the cabbage,
a few tbsp. of water,
one spoonful vinegar,
and a pinch of salt.
Cover and simmer for
30 minutes over a moderate
heat. Slice the apples thinly,
add to the cabbage and return
to the heat until the apples are
cooked. Finally, add the sugar
and simmer, without a lid,
until the excess juice
has evaporated.
I cannot resist the temptation
to give you a recipe used
for our lunch with Madame
de Nicolaÿ. It is an unusual,
but delicious, starter.
Prepare some fresh broad beans,
cooking them for a few minutes
until tender. Leave to cool.
Meanwhile, make a vinaigrette
flavoured with very finely-
chopped shallots. Remove the
outer skin from the broad beans.
Just before serving, blend the
broad beans and vinaigrette with
a small jar of black lump eggs.
This is a sure winner!

At Le Lude, after Mass on Christmas Eve, the children's menu was as follows:

Consommé with Poached Eggs
Fillet of Beef with Russian Salad
Chocolate Cream Dessert

At Le Lude, after Mass on Christmas Eve, the parents' menu was as follows:

Strasbourg Foie Gras with Truffles
Aiguillette with Beef
Cold Jellied Chicken
Chocolate Gâteau

" Champagne was not then a tradition at the end of the meal. The only wine was a sweet, mellow Château d'Yquem."
As to the famous Fanchonnettes, the little vanilla cream tarts topped with a white or golden mousse and a soupçon of red-currant jam, we do not have the recipe because it disappeared when the chef who made them died.

Seen from the terrace overlooking the River Loir, the massive towers on the south side of the Château du Lude are reminiscent of Chambord; on the east side, the façade is in the Classical Louis XVI style.

MONTGEOFFROY

A Maréchal with a taste for good food

———◆———

Flan tins, biscuit tins, patty tins etc. all laid out on the 18th-century kitchen table made of ash.

Two hundred and sixty copper kitchen utensils (or perhaps more - we did not recount them) line the walls of the kitchen in Montgeoffroy. A chef's dream, a collection built up over several decades and each item has its own particular use. There are saucepans, a range of moulds, tiny biscuit tins, ice cream makers etc. A complete set of utensils, all lined up in battle order, in the kitchen that once belonged to a Maréchal. If châteaux are usually linked to a lengthy history, Montgeoffroy is rather more connected with a person with enormous strength of character - Louis-Georges-Erasme de Contades, Maréchal de France and Knight of the Orders of the King.

It was in 1772 that the Maréchal de Contades ordered the demolition of the 16th-century family seat, retaining only the two towers and the chapel. After a brilliant career that had taken him to Corsica, Flanders and Germany, and after having governed Alsace, the Maréchal wanted to retire to a residence that befitted his rank. At the age of sixty-eight, he commissioned the construction of a large Classical château from a Parisian architect named Barré, whose style was a continuation of Gabriel's work. The château was completed in just four years. Everything was planned to the last detail, including the timber used for eighteen identical commodes in various rooms - rosewood on the

This 19th-century plate-warmer worked on embers.

piano nobile and fruit tree wood for the upper storey. There was even a dining room, a great novelty for the time. The Château de Montgeoffroy was rational and well-planned, richly-furnished and decorated. It still looks as it did when first built and is a fine example of the Louis XVI style. In fact, the Maréchal spent very little time there, since he retained his functions in Strasbourg and at court. It was he who carried the crown of France during Louis XVI's coronation in 1775. He refused to emigrate when the French Revolution broke out and, instead, sought refuge with his good friends, the Misses Hérault de Séchelles (for whom he had an apartment laid out in Montgeoffroy, overlooking the garden), and died there in 1795 "after a violent argument with his servants"! The art of warfare, his love of foie gras and an imperious character had nevertheless taken him to the ripe old age of ninety-two! Since there, Montgeoffroy has always remained in the same family and we were welcomed by Arnold, Marquis de Contades, and his wife who gave us a selection of recipes old and new.

In this oval "dining room", an alcove was built to hold the Strasbourg ceramic stove given to the Maréchal by the town. The French East India Company plates came from his father-in-law, Magon de La Lande, a shipowner in Saint-Malo.

AUG. MICHEL
Fabrique de Pâtés de Foies Gras
STRASBOURG-SCHILTIGHEIM
(Alsace)

PÂTÉ DE FOIE GRAS DIT PÂTÉ DE STRASBOURG

Foie Gras Paté

Serves 10 - 12:

Stuffing

375 g fillet of pork

175 g fresh streaky bacon

125 g parings of uncooked
foie gras - 25 g spiced salt

Pound all the ingredients
together and pass through
a sieve. Complete the stuffing
with the marinade used for the
liver. The paté requires a good
firm goose liver weighing
700 - 800 g stuck with quarters
of uncooked truffles, seasoned
with spiced salt and marinated
3 hours in advance in 10 cl
cognac and 10 cl madeira.
Line a cylindrical mould
(diameter approximately 12 cm -
5 inches) with 1 kg very firm
pastry that has been allowed
to rest. Line the base and sides
with some of the stuffing.
Lay the liver in the middle and
cover with the remainder of the
stuffing. On the top, place a
strip of streaky bacon, a pinch
of spices, and a bay leaf. Cover
with a pastry "lid" and decorate.
Make a funnel in the centre of
the paté to let steam escape
during cooking. Brush with milk
or egg yolk. Cook in the oven
(180 °C) for approximately
45 minutes. When the paté
is cold, fill up with aspic.

To serve

Remove the pastry "lid" and
serve the foie gras in the form
of quenelles scooped out
with a spoon.

*One day, Maréchal de Contades
tired of foie gras, that great
Alsatian speciality. In its place,
his chef, Clause, created an unusual
recipe for which we are indebted
to Viviane and Antoine
Westermann. It can be tasted in
their restaurant and in the home
of the two privileged persons to
whom they send some at Christmas,
the Marquis de Contades and
Her Majesty Queen Elizabeth II.*

CRÈME DE CRESSON

Watercress Cream Soup

Put a generous spoonful of butter to melt in a pan over a high
heat. When it almost begins to
burn, add the washed watercress,
which reduces by three-quarters.
Add some salt before stirring, and
pour in 2 litres cold water. Leave
on a high heat until boiling.

Meanwhile, peel, wash and dry three medium-sized potatoes. Cut them in quarters then slice thinly. Add to the watercress. Cook over a low heat. When the potatoes are cooked, put the ingredients in a food blender and blend until the green leaves have disappeared. Heat up a soup tureen, pour in 50 cl preheated crème fraîche and add the watercress soup. Stir until smooth and serve very hot.

After tasting this seven hour leg of lamb in Montgeoffroy, the Queen Mother asked the chef to come to Windsor Castle to give the chefs there the recipe.

LE GIGOT D'AGNEAU DE MONTGEOFFROY

Montgeoffroy-style Leg of Lamb

The Château de Montgeoffroy has a small sheep farm which produces the lambs for this delicious recipe, the seven hour leg of lamb.

Lay the leg of lamb in a long, deep dish, pour on several spoonfuls of olive oil and brush over the entire piece of meat. Add one bottle dry white wine, one sliced carrot, a thinly-sliced onion, some thyme, bay and a few unpeeled cloves of garlic. Leave to marinate overnight, turning the meat two or three times. Put some oil on a baking tray the size of the leg of lamb and brown the meat on both sides. Then add the marinade and some stock until it reaches halfway up the meat. Place in an oven on a low heat and leave to cook for 7 hours without covering the meat. Serve in the cooking tray.

En l'honneur de S.M. la reine mère d'Angleterre
déjeuner à Montgeoffroy le vendredi 15 mai 1981

Duc et Duchesse de Grafton
Lady Fermoy
Sir Ralph Amstrather bt
Prince Jean Louis de Faucigny. Lucinge
Prince et Princesse Armand d'Aremberg
Prince et Princesse de Ligne la Tremoïlle

Filets de Sole farcie
au poivre vert

Gigot de 7 heures

Feuilletés aux fruits rouge
Sorbet à l'orange

Le vendredi 15 mai 1981

Elizabeth R

Mai 15th
1981

Pheasant Paté.

TERRINE DE FAISAN

Pheasant Paté

After plucking and drawing the pheasant, clean the offal and set aside.

Bone the pheasant and keep the fillets. Marinate them in brandy for 2 hours. Mince the pheasant meat, 250 g pork hock, 250 g lean veal, one onion and some parsley. Mix the minced ingredients with some thyme, one glass of white wine, salt and pepper. Drain the pheasant fillets. Add the brandy to the minced ingredients. Line the terrine with pork fat, place one-half of the stuffing on top (if it is too liquid, add an egg, mixing well) then the pheasant fillets. Cover with the remainder of the stuffing. Garnish with a few slices of carrot and some small sprigs of parsley. Cover the paté dish.

Prepare a bain-marie, place the terrine in it and cook in a moderate oven for 2 hours. Leave until cold. Fill with madeira aspic and put in a cool place for 24 hours.

SALADE ESTIVALE

Summer Salad

One of the Marquise de Contades' own recipes

Cook some Di Ceco pasta *al dente* in salted water. Rinse well under cold water to prevent further cooking. Pour over some groundnut oil so that it does not become sticky. Set aside. In a bowl, macerate adequate quantities of olive oil, groundnut oil, paprika, strong pimento, one or two small birds-eye peppers (halved) and some chopped basil leaves. Taste. Cut some mozzarella into small cubes. Peel tomatoes, remove the pips and dice the flesh. Fry some very thin slices of smoked streaky bacon until well-cooked but not burnt. Dry on absorbent kitchen paper. Stone some black olives and cut into two or three pieces. Add a few to macerate in the sauce. Mix all the ingredients with the pasta. Add some whole fresh basil leaves and decorate with mozzarella.

ŒUFS POCHÉS AU VIN ROUGE

Eggs Poached in Red Wine

Put some water to boil with 2 tbsp. vinegar. Meanwhile, fill a saucepan with cold water. Break the egg and slip it gently into the simmering water for 3 minutes then remove and put in the cold water. Drain on a teatowel. Repeat for the required

number of eggs, adding
a little vinegar each time.

Red Wine Sauce (serves 4)
Sweat three thinly-sliced shallots
in some clarified butter.
Add 40 cl red wine, bring
to the boil and reduce by
two-thirds then deglaze.
Add four spoonfuls of single
cream. Beat with a whisk
and again reduce by one-quarter. Make the sauce with
150 g softened butter. Put back
on the heat but do not allow
to boil. Stir to ensure that
the sauce is smooth then season
with salt and pepper.
Put the eggs back in the boiling
water for thirty seconds to reheat
them. Lay them on hot plates,
pour the sauce over the top
and dot with chopped chives.

Sauté de veau

Veal Stew

Serves 10

3 kg veal cut into pieces
(hock, kernel).
Cut six carrots and three onions
into four, or chop roughly.
Wipe but do not wash.
Put some oil in a stew pan
and sweat the vegetables over a
moderate heat with an unpeeled
head of garlic. Add a calf's foot.
Season the uncooked meat with
salt and pepper, dust lightly with
flour and brown on all sides
in a frying pan containing

one-half oil and one-half butter.
Once the meat has browned,
drain and deglaze the frying pan
with 50 cl white wine. Add the
veal to the stew pan containing
the vegetables, with 2 tbsp.
tomato puree and four fresh
tomatoes (quartered). Add the
deglazing liquid, a clove, some
thyme and bay. The wine should
reduce by one-half, over a high
heat. Cover with chicken stock
(or a stock cube). Bring to the
boil over a high heat, skim, then
cover the pan and simmer gently
for approximately 2 hours.

Copper and zinc,
a harmonious display.

A beautiful copper tap
in one of the kitchens.

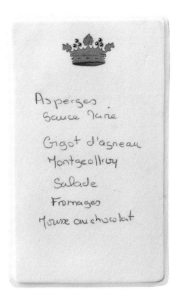

Asperges
Sauce Marie

Gigot d'agneau
Montgeoffroy

Salade

Fromages

Mousse au chocolat

These copper pans have countless stories to tell. They have been repaired and regalvanised many times but are still ready for use.

MOUSSE DE CAFÉ LÉGÈRE

Light Coffee Mousse

Put eight egg yolks and
125 g sugar in a mixer bowl
and beat until white then add
3 tbsp. coffee extract.
Taste. Pour the coffee cream
into a mixing bowl.
Pour 75 cl cream
into the mixer bowl
and whip until stiff.
Mix the whipped cream
into the coffee cream a little
at a time, starting from the
middle and using a rubber
spatula until there is no more
cream left.
To mix, fold the cream in.
Place in the fridge
for at least 1 hour.
Garnish with little biscuits
and chopped almonds.

COQUILLES SAINT-JACQUES SUR LIT D'ENDIVES

Scallops on a Bed of Chicory

Prepare five scallops per person.
Melt some butter and, when
it is nut brown, fry the scallops
al dente then season with salt
and pepper. Set aside.
Wash and finely slice the
chicory. Season slightly with a
light vinaigrette. Lay out a bed
of chicory and arrange the
scallops over the top.
Pour on a little lemon juice
and dot with sprigs of chervil.

TARTE TATIN

Upside-down Apple Tart

*Marie, the cook at Montgeoffroy,
thought her apple tart was too
dark for the photo so she
made us another one.
We selected the first one -
and ate both!*

Peel 2 kg russet apples.
Cut into quarters and remove
the core. Dampen a sponge tin,
grease well with butter,
and sprinkle on some castor
sugar. Lay the apple quarters
across the base. Put in a hot
oven until the apples begin to
colour. Meanwhile, prepare
some shortcrust pastry and leave
to rest for 1 hour.
Take the tin out
of the oven and place
the shortcrust over the top,
tucking it down the sides.
Cook in a hot oven for
approximately 30 minutes.

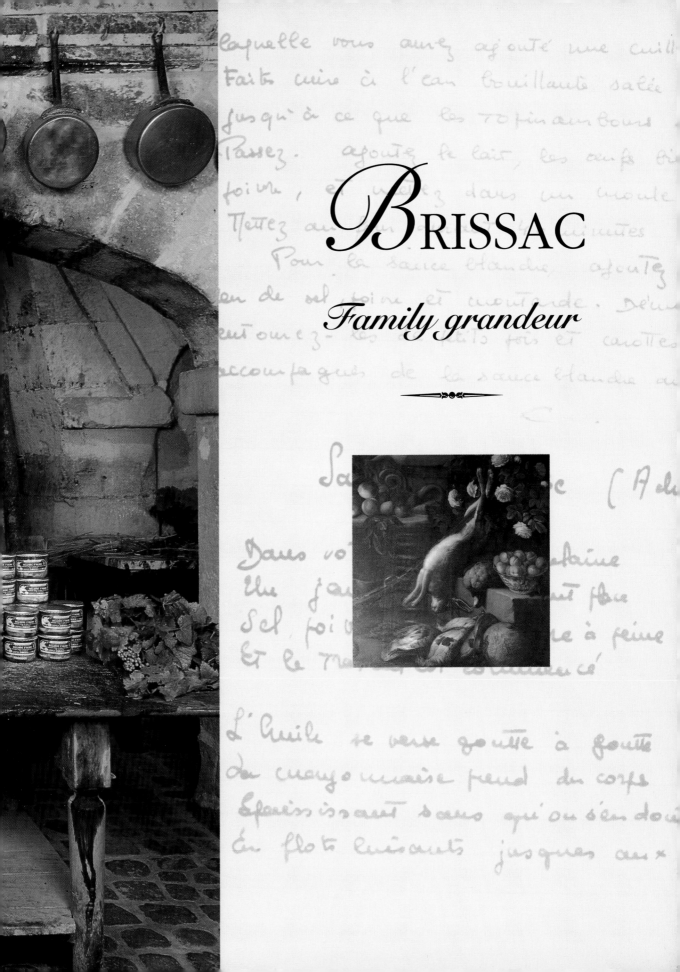

BRISSAC
Family grandeur

*E*verything in this, the tallest château in France, is large. The staircase is monumental, the guardroom is vast, and the kitchens large enough to feed an entire garrison. We asked the Grand Master, Charles-André de Brissac, to pose with two members of the Confrérie des Rillauds, a brotherhood which holds gargantuan meetings in honour of good food and good wine. The kitchen is in a seven-storey pavilion overlooking the River Aubance, the river that flows through the vineyards of Anjou. The Cossé family has lived in Brissac since 1502 and has taken the name of the château. On the death of Duc Pierre, the title passed to his son, François, whose eldest son,

The paintings decorating the dining room were part of a Nicolaÿ legacy from the Château de Bercy. It was replaced by narrow streets filled with wine merchants' premises; they, in their turn, were demolished.

Charles-André, is a Marquis. Such are the titles in this family.

The first castle was built by the de Brézé family. Nothing remains of it today except the two round towers on the façade. In 1601, Charles II de Cossé demolished the castle and commissioned the building of a tall construction. In fact, it was never built and the two old towers remained adjacent to each other as if waiting for a demolition squad that never seems to arrive.

From the outset, the Brissacs have held high office. When Francis I, captured after his defeat at the Battle of Pavia, exchanged his own freedom in return for the use of his sons as hostages by arrangement with Emperor Charles V, the royal offspring were accompanied into exile by two members of the Brissac family. Their descendant, Charles, was Maréchal of France, as was his brother Artus and his son. It was the latter, Charles II, who was raised to the dukedom in 1611, thereby becoming a peer of the realm, and he who carried out alterations to the château. His grandson, who was both Duc and Maréchal, left some outstanding interior refurbishments, bringing into juxtaposition enormous chambers (the guardroom is 32 metres - 104 ft. in length) and apartments decorated with an eye to luxury. There is, of course, a king's bedchamber in which Louis XIII and his mother, Marie de Médicis, were reconciled in 1620. There is even a theatre on the second floor, inaugurated in 1890 and still used to this day.

To illustrate Brissac, we naturally chose the grand dining room with the admirable Meissen porcelain and the Sèvres service bearing the coat-of-arms of the Brissacs, "of sable a three fasces or alias argent, indented at the base".

Small pots with the Brissac cipher. "Virtute Tempore", the family motto.

...he was a Barbe-Ponsardin by birth but was better-known as Veuve (or Widow) Clicquot. Michel Dovaz wrote, "No other Frenchwoman except Joan of Arc is as famous as she is in foreign countries". Widowed at the age of twenty-seven, this woman succeeded in regrouping land in Champagne to turn it into a large vineyard and in developing a company that still bears her name to this day. Her great-granddaughter was Duchesse d'Uzès and master of the hounds; she was one of the Cossé-Brissac family's ancestors.

"François de Brissac was so fond of russet apples that, when he wanted to praise something, he always added the words to the end of his sentence eg. He was as honest as a russet apple".
From the portrait of the second Duke in the Historiettes written by Tallemand des Réaux.

LES RILLAUDS

The word "rillaud"
comes from an old
16th-century French word,
"rille" meaning "strip
of streaky bacon".
Rillauds d'Anjou are pieces
of pork cooked in stock made
with pork bones,
aromatic herbs and tasty
vegetables. They take hours
to cook then, when the stock
has reduced well, pork fat
or lard is added
and the cooking continues.
Hot "rillauds" are served
with potatoes fried
in goose fat or with
a green salad.
They can also be eaten
very cold.

Menu for a return from the hunt

After the Hunt Soup
Pheasant Szechenyi
Plum Pie

*In the hallway of the Château de Brissac,
there are reminders that this is a great
hunting family. This one was caught in 1919.*

BOUILLON
RETOUR DE CHASSE

After the Hunt Soup

Take a wild rabbit, an old
partridge, two or three quail.
Pluck, draw, flame etc.
then place in a pot with a slice
of ham. Pour on water and a
bottle of madeira. Bring to the
boil, skim and season like
an ordinary stew.
Simmer over a low heat for
4 hours then clarify. Puree
the flesh from the game and
taste to ensure that it does not
lack salt. Put some croûtons
in the soup tureen and pour
over the very hot soup.
Melt a knob of good butter
in the game puree and
pour onto the soup just
before serving.
To clarify the soup:
Slip an egg white into the soup.
As it coagulates,
it traps any impurities.
This is the same principle
as "collage" used in
wine-making.

FAISAN SZECHENYI

Pheasant Szechenyi

In honour of an ancestor of Larissa de Brissac née Szechenyi who worked to achieve Hungarian independence.

Wash a good green cabbage (halved). Blanch in boiling water then drain and press well to remove all the water from the leaves. Set aside. Peel a few potatoes (the number depends on the number of guests). Slice thinly, put in cold water and set to one side. Prepare the pheasant: pluck, draw and clean.

Bring some water to the boil. Clean a fresh foie gras and plunge into the simmering water for 20 minutes. Drain and carefully dry. Season with salt and pepper, add some paprika on all sides and stuff the pheasant with it. Set the pheasant in an ovenproof dish with slices of bacon in the base. Grease lightly with oil and butter. Cook for an hour.

Cut a few peppers of different colours (red, green, yellow etc.) into thin strips and cook gently in olive oil. Butter a charlotte mould and line with well-pressed cabbage leaves. Season alternately with salt and pepper. Cover with slices of bacon and place in the oven to the left of the pheasant. Butter some patty tins or small pancake pans and arrange the slices of potato in them, after wiping them dry. Season with salt and pepper and add a little oil and butter so that they cook properly. Place to the right of the pheasant if your oven is large enough. The pheasant will be cooked in 1 hour, as will the garnishes. Cut the game and foie gras, remove the cabbage

"This is the bushel and standard of the lord of Brissac". These words run right round the standard bushel bearing the family crest, a fiscal measurement used in the 16th century.

charlotte from the mould and the roast potatoes from the tin. Add the strips of pepper to the serving dish.

PÂTÉ AUX PRUNES

Plum Pie

Plum Pie is a speciality of Anjou where it is made with greengages in honour of Claude of France, wife of Francis I and daughter of Anne of Brittany, since a greengage is called "reine-claude" in French.

Make some shortcrust pastry, divide in half and leave it to rest. Make a sugar and water syrup and put the stoned greengages in the syrup for a couple of minutes. Line a round tin with one half of the pastry, arrange the fruit on top with some sugar, and cover with the other half of the pastry. Make a funnel in the middle and brush with egg. Bake in the oven until cooked.

TERRINE DE CHEVREUIL

Venison Paté

The hunt known as the Rallye Châtelaine, which has as its master of the hounds the Duc de Brissac, hunts roe deer. This is the most difficult form of hunting; it requires dogs with a good sense of smell and a high degree of subtlety.

Here is a recipe that uses various pieces of the meat. Roughly mince 800 g venison. Mince more finely 300 g lean pork (loin or fillet) and 300 g fatty bacon. Place in a basin and mix in one egg, a small glass of cognac, 100 g whole hazelnuts, a little tarragon, salt and pepper. Line a terrine with pork fat and press in the mixture, decorating with crossed strips of pork fat. Put in a bain-marie in the oven and cook for 2 hours at a moderate heat. Wait for at least 24 hours before eating.

An 18th-century Sèvres soup tureen bearing the Brissac coat-of-arms.

SAUMON DE LOIRE À L'OSEILLE

Loire Salmon with Sorrel

A good-sized salmon can be cut into steaks 2 cm - approx. 1 inch thick. Cook the steaks in a well-flavoured stock coloured with a few drops of wine vinegar. The stock should have simmered for at least one hour in a covered pan before the salmon steaks are cooked in it. Turn off the heat and leave the fish to cook naturally, with the pan still covered, while you prepare the sorrel sauce. Slice the sorrel leaves thinly and drop into a small quantity of water.
Add a spoonful of crème fraîche and chilled butter in small pieces. Blend with a whisk but do not allow to boil or the sauce will lose its smoothness. Season with salt and pepper. Set aside in a bain-marie. Remove the salmon steaks from the cooking stock and lay on a white cloth. They should be well wiped. Lay them out on a silver platter and pour the sauce over the top. Serve with boiled rice or boiled potatoes.

COTIGNAC

Quince Jujubes

Take the best quince you can find and remove the cores. Do not peel the fruit - most of the bouquet and special flavour of the quince is to be found in the skin. Remove the pips and the fibrous part then put the fruit in a preserving pan of water, turning it from time to time with a wooden spoon until it is soft. Remove from the water and place in a sieve over a terrine. When the quince have cooled, mash and reduce to a pulp. Reduce the pulp by one-half over the heat then remove the preserving pan from the heat and pour the mixture into a glazed earthenware jar or into a terrine. This is a precaution that cannot be too highly

recommended. Clarify the same quantity of sugar and quince mixture and cook to a slow rolling boil, stirring well with a wooden spoon as you pour in the quince. When the mixture has blended well, put the preserving pan back on a low heat, stirring continuously until the base of the pan is clearly visible, then remove the pan from the heat. On a metal tray or slates, stand moulds of various shapes (circles, squares, heart shapes) and fill them with the mixture taking care to even off the surface with a knife. When all the moulds have been filled, sprinkle with sugar and place in a well-heated drying oven. Two days later, remove from the moulds, turn over and place on a sieve then sprinkle with sugar on the second side. Leave them as they are for one day in the drying oven. Store in well-sealed tins, in layers separated by sheets of plain white paper.

Alexandre Dumas, author of The Hunchback of Notre-Dame, also quotes this old recipe which is also mentioned by Grimod de La Reynière. Tallemand des Réaux, however, speaks of it much earlier during rivalry between Francis I and Maréchal de Brissaç for the love of a lady.

"A new château half-built in an old castle half-demolished". This definition was given by Pierre, twelfth Duc de Brissac.

GOULAINE

Oh kitchens, oh châteaux

Robert and Gudrun
de Goulain
in the château's
age-old cellars.
Above: "To this one,
to that one,
I grant crowns."

A few years ago, Robert de Goulaine had already talked to us about his wish to re-open the cellars that run underneath the entire central part of the château. Now he has done so. Clearing the rubble was no easy task but the cellars, which date from the earliest castle, can now be used for wine-tasting in the company of this leading connoisseur of wines from all over the world - and, of course, for the presentation of the Château de Goulaine's own Muscadet. The Goulaine family has been producing wine for almost one thousand years in the Nantes area. The family tree has been detailed back to the 12th century and includes several famous names including Mathieu, the son of Jean I (the first member of the acknowledged family tree), who brought about conciliation between England and France. In return, he received the unique privilege of bearing the arms of both sovereigns, the leopards of England and lilies of France. The family motto is reminiscent of this arbitration procedure, "To this one, to that one, I grant the crowns". It can be seen on the dormer windows along the façade, abbreviated to AAA (*"A cestuy-ci, A cestuy-là, j'Accorde les Couronnes"*). From their castle, the Goulaines used to look out over a vast estate that comprised much of the current Muscadet-growing territory in Sèvre-et-Maine; it was raised to a marquisate by Henry IV. However, a quirk of history led to the sale of Goulaine in 1788. A happier turn of events led to its being

repurchased in 1858. Robert, Marquis de Goulaine, who lives in the château on a permanent basis, is the twenty-ninth generation of an eminent (and food-loving) family. The family notebooks that he showed us are ample proof of this fact. Flower-based meals, mystery dishes - the kitchen knows how to surprise or be elegant. It is eclectic, too, a reflection of European aristocracy thanks to its many alliances and marriages. We have selected a German recipe supplied by the Marquise de Goulaine, and an Ecuadorian recipe supplied by Janeth, the wife of Mathieu who represents the thirtieth generation. And of course, there is the chestnut-filled "Goulaine Log". Not forgetting Clémence, the château's cook at the beginning of the century, who invented the famous White Butter Sauce here before making it popular in her inn on the banks of the Loire. The origins of great recipes are often open to question but this one has been confirmed by numerous authors, of which Curnonsky was the first.

While on the subject of butter, the archives in Nantes have an early 17th-century document which mentions a load of four tonnes of butter passing through the toll-gate in the harbour bound for the harbour at Goulaine. The ship's captain refused to pay the harbour dues on the grounds that "the cargo is for the Marquis de Goulaine's personal consumption". His argument with the harbourmaster stretches over almost twenty pages and everything has been conscientiously reported! This epic battle of words was won by the ship's captain who left Nantes without paying the dues! The Marquis liked butter; so did his large household.

The private dining room.

LE CEVICHE

A recipe supplied
by Janeth de Goulaine,
the Marquis' daughter-in-law,
who comes from Ecuador.

This dish is served
in a bowl and eaten cold
with a spoon as a starter.
It is a deliciously refreshing dish
that needs to be
well-seasoned with pimento.
Ingredients:

1 kg large shelled prawns,
preferably from Ecuador
7 very ripe tomatoes (diced)
A large quantity of fresh
coriander leaves (chopped)
2 onions (thinly-sliced)
Use all the ingredients to make
the sauce. Mix two tomatoes
in a blender, collect the juice
and add the juice of three
lemons and one orange,
two tbsp. olive oil, some salt
and two pinches of pimento
(or more, if liked).
The "ceviche" is to Ecuador
what gaspacho is to Spain.
The dish is served with green
banana crisps: thinly slice
green bananas and fry
in a deep fat fryer.
The crisps should be - crisp!
Ceviche can also be eaten
with popcorn, but green
bananas are better.

GÂTEAU D'ANNIVERSAIRE

Birthday Cake

Serves 8:
Make the praline first.
Place a heavy-bottomed,
non-galvanised frying
pan over a high heat
and put in it 125 g castor sugar
and an equal quantity
of almonds in their skins.
Do not add any liquid.
Stir over the heat
until the sugar has turned
into brown brittle
toffee. Pour onto an oiled
marble slab or tiled working
surface. When the toffee
has cooled, crush with
a pestle and mortar or grate
with a potato peeler.

Then make the sponge:
Beat 100 g sugar and four eggs
over a low heat.
Remove from the heat
and mix in 75 g praline,
80 g flour and 50 g melted
butter. Pour into a buttered,
greased sponge tin and bake
in a low oven for 45 minutes
then remove from the tin
and leave to cool.
Meanwhile, prepare a cream
filling with two egg whites,
100 g sugar, 100 g butter
and the remainder
of the praline. Beat the egg
whites and sugar over a gentle
heat then remove from the heat
and leave to cool.
When almost cold,
add the butter and praline.
Cut the sponge into two
or three layers, spread the cream
filling on the layers and
sandwich back together again.

Fondant icing
Fondant icing should be made
in advance; it can be kept

Goulaine Log.

for some time
without spoiling.
Using a frying pan as indicated
above, cook 1 lb. loaf sugar
over a high heat with half
a glass of hot water.
Cook until the syrup begins
to bubble. Pour the syrup
onto a marble slab.
When it no longer sticks
to the fingers, work it
with a spatula until you obtain
a firm, white paste which should
then be worked by hand
until all the lumps have been
removed. Take one-half
of the fondant to ice the cake
and place over a low heat
with a spoonful of rum.
Stir well then pour onto the cake
while still very hot.
Spread it quickly with a palette
knife and leave to dry.

Icing decorations

150 g loaf sugar, a spoonful
of vinegar. Mix in a copper pan
and cook until a small piece
of the sugar syrup breaks easily
when dropped into cold water.
Pour onto the oiled marble
slab when warm and work it
by pulling out and refolding
until it is firm but still pliant.
At this point, you can use it as
you want, to make flowers,
candleholders, little bows etc.
By mixing in red
and green food colourings
while it is still hot and on the
marble slab, you can obtain
some splendid effects.

Wording

5 tsp. icing sugar in
a very small quantity
of egg white and a few drops
of lemon juice.

Bûche
GOULAINE

Goulaine Log

Ingredients:
  500 g chestnut puree
  75 g castor sugar
  125 g butter
  1 tsp. vanilla sugar
  2 bars chocolate
  (grated)
Mix all the ingredients
well by hand in a mixing
 bowl. Form into
a log shape and place
on a long dish.
To ice, melt the two bars
of chocolate in two spoonfuls
of water with a knob
of butter, or decorate
with almonds, walnuts
and hazelnuts

LES FRAISES AU MELON

Strawberries with Melon

*A recipe sent
by G.R. de Salles to his friend,
Ch. Monselet*

When the chimes ring out for
the melons and for the delicate
little alpine strawberries
that have such taste,
here is what you must
do if you want to have
in your mouth all the flowers
of this terrestrial paradise.
Take a Cavaillon melon.
Using a knife with a silver-gilt
blade, make a circular incision
around the stalk. Once you have
opened the fruit, use a silver
spoon to remove the pips,
taking care not to mark the
flesh. Having completed
this initial duty with the respect
demanded of such a task,
pour into the belly of the melon
two spoonfuls of excellent
refined sugar. On this soft bed,
arrange a layer of strawberries
and continue to build up
the layers in the same way until
the melon is full. Then uncork a
bottle of "irreproachable" claret
and pour it into the darling
melon to fill up any empty
spaces left by the sugar and
fruit. Having done this, reseal
the melon with the part you first
removed. Carry it to your coolest
cellar and leave it to marinate
for 24 hours. After this, the
solemn moment will have arrived. Pour into a fruit bowl the
contents of the melon and
savour every mouthful. As to the
melon itself, you can give it to a
four-legged friend who will be
sure to enjoy it. And now,
I shake your hand and pray God
that he keep you
in opulent health.
Yours in heart and stomach.

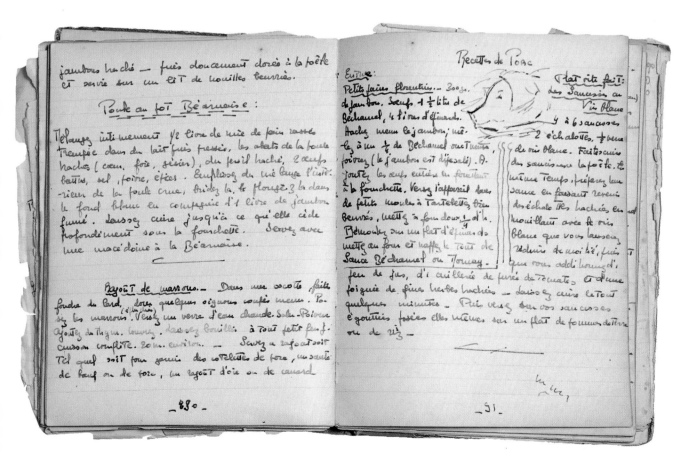

GÂTEAU AU FROMAGE BLANC

Cheesecake

*Made by the Marquise
de Goulaine.*

Mix 200 g flour, 1 level tsp.
baking powder, 75 g sugar,
1 tsp. vanilla sugar, one egg
and 75 g butter.
Roll out to fit a sponge tin
with sides 4 cm
(almost 2 inches) high.
Mix 750 g fromage frais,
150 g sugar, 1 tsp. vanilla sugar,
5 tbsp. cornflour, four egg yolks,
and the grated rind
of one lemon. Add the stiffly-
beaten egg whites.
Fill the pastry case in the cake
tin with the mixture and bake
for 1 hour at 175 °C.

The Question Mark Menu

Two mystery dishes…

ŒUFS EN SURPRISE

Surprise Eggs

Empty the eggshells by piercing
each end of the shell
with a large needle.
Prepare a cheese sauce
and fill the shells with a tiny
pharmaceutical funnel or a small
spoon. Close off the ends with
sealing wax or with a circle
of paper glued in place with
a flour and water paste. Cook
the eggs in a bain-marie and
in the oven or in the bain-marie
only, for 20 to 30 minutes.

The water should come at least
halfway up the eggs,
with the end having the largest
hole being kept out of the water
(put the eggs in egg cups or in
a specially-made egg basket).

Cheese Sauce

For 3 or 4 eggs:
50 cl milk, pepper, salt
if possible 30-40 g grated cheese
nutmeg or any other
flavouring e.g.
a few drops
of truffle
or mushroom essence

FRITTURA MYSTÈRE

Mystery Fritters

Prepare a quantity of fritter
batter. Also prepare all sorts
of different fillings:
- seasonal vegetables
(or canned or frozen vegetables)
in small pieces (sprigs
of cauliflower, small tender
artichokes prepared
and quartered, salsify,
carrots or turnips, Chinese
artichokes, slices of aubergines
or Jerusalem artichokes,
whole or chopped mushrooms);
- shellfish (remove sand
and shell) taken with a spoon
(mussels, cockles etc.);
- fresh, canned or frozen fish
fillets;
- pieces of meat e.g. strips
of liver, pieces of kidney,
slices of cooked sausage,
sausages, etc.
- hard-boiled eggs (quartered),
pieces of cheese etc.
Heat the oil until it begins
to smoke, being careful not to
fry too many fritters at one time.
With each new batch,
add a few sprigs of parsley
in the oil to remove the smell
or taste of strong-flavoured
fish or foods.
To serve, build up a pyramid
of various types of fritters.
Decorate with sprigs of parsley.

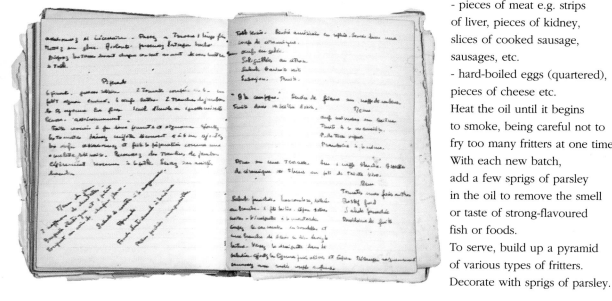

*F*lower Dinners

DAHLIAS EN SALADE

Dahlia Salad

Wash the tubers and cook in boiling salted water. Peel then slice and season with salt, pepper and vinegar while still hot. Add a generous quantity of pepper to offset the very mild, sweet taste of the tuber.

BEIGNET DE CHRYSANTHÈMES

Chrysanthemum Fritter

Wash the petals of ordinary yellow chrysanthemums. Dry, then dip into a crisp fritter batter (the batter made with beer is very good for this; if you make your batter with egg, add a little brandy and a spoonful of oil). Fry in a deep fat fryer and build up a light pyramid to serve, with cayenne pepper in a pepper pot on the side.

SALADE DE CAPUCINES

Nasturtium Salad

Serve on a base of well-drained cooked spinach.

Although Goulaine is in Brittany, its architectural style and the use of Saumur tuff makes it the last in the long line of Loire Valley châteaux.

FLAN D'ŒILLETS BLANCS

Carnation Flan

Cook some white carnation petals for a few minutes in milk and sugar. Stirring continuously, add the milk and petals to eggs beaten with a little flour (2 tbsp. flour and 2 eggs per half-litre of milk). Cook in a bain-marie or in the oven in soufflé dishes (cooking time: approximately 20 minutes). N.B. This flan is arguably even better as a savoury dish than as a sweet. In this case, add a generous quantity of pepper.

Practical information

1. Château de La Buissière-45230 La Buissière

MH. Member VMF and DH.
Open end of March to 11th November: vegetable garden, château, river angling collections.
Owner: Madame de Chasseval
Phone: 02 38 35 93 35

2. Château de La Ferté-Saint-Aubin - 45240 La Ferté-Saint-Aubin

MH. Member VMF and DH.
Open 15th March to 15th November: château, grounds, stables.
Cookery demonstrations, annual exhibitions.
Owner: Monsieur Jacques Guyot.
Phone: 02 38 76 52 72
Fax: 02 38 64 67 43

3. Château de Beauregard - 41120 Cellettes

MH since 1840 (château).
ISMH Grounds and outhouses. Member VMF and DH.
Château and grounds open all year except January.
Tour of Portraits Garden, May to October.
Reception rooms available for weddings, seminars, and party functions.
Owner: Madame du Pavillon
Phone: 02 54 70 40 05
Fax: 02 54 70 36 74

4. Château de Chenonceau - 37150 Chenonceaux

MH. Member of DH.
Open all year. Waxworks museum. Restaurants.
Receptions and seminars. Sound and light show, July and August.
Owner: Menier family
Curator: Mr. Bernard Voisin
Phone: 02 47 23 90 07
Fax: 02 47 23 80 88
Restaurant chef: Mr. Jacky Tisseron

5. Château de Villandry - 37510 Villandry

MH: grounds and château.
Member of DH.
Château and gardens open all year.
Owner: Monsieur Carvallo
Phone: 02 47 50 02 09
Fax: 02 47 50 12 85

6. Château des Réaux - 37140 Chouze-sur-Loire

ISMH. Member of VMF and DH.
Open all year for parties. B&B and table d'hôte.
Owners: Monsieur and Madame Goupil de Bouillé
Phone: 02 47 95 14 40
Fax: 02 47 95 18 34

7. Château d'Ussé - 37420 Rigny-Ussé.

MH. Member of DH.
Open February to 11th November: château, chapel, cellars, terraced gardens designed by Le Nôtre.
Costume exhibition.
Sleeping Beauty exhibition.
Owner: Monsieur de Blacas
Phone: 02 47 95 54 05
Fax: 02 47 95 41 02

8. Château de Montreuil-Bellay - 49260 Montreuil-Bellay

MH. Member of VMH and DH.
Open 1st April to 1st November.
Owners: Monsieur and Madame de Thuy
Phone: 02 41 52 33 06
Fax: 02 41 52 37 70

9. Château de Lude - 72800 Le Lude

MH. Member of VMH and DH.
Open 1st April to 30th September (by prior arrangement in low season): château, outbuildings and gardens (gardeners' weekend, first weekend in June). Sound and light show in summer.
Owner: Monsieur L-J. de Nicolaÿ
Phone: 02 43 94 60 09
Fax: 02 43 45 27 53

10. Château de Montgeoffroy - 49250 Mazé

MH. Member of VMF and DH.
Open from Palm Sunday to 1st November.
Antiques Fair.
Owner: Monsieur de Contades
Phone: 02 41 80 60 02
Fax: 02 41 80 62 66

11. Château de Brissac - 49320 Brissac

MH. Member of VMF and DH.
Open April to October.
Receptions and meals. WIne-tasting.
Owner: Monsieur de Cossé-Brissac
Phone: 02 41 91 22 21
Fax: 02 41 91 25 60

12. Château de Goulaine - 44115 Haute-Goulaine

MH. Member of VMF and DH
Open end of March to early November (open all year for parties): château, butterfly house.
Receptions, weddings, seminars. Wine-tasting.
Owner: Monsieur Robert de Goulaine
Phone: 02 40 54 91 42
Fax: 02 40 54 90 23

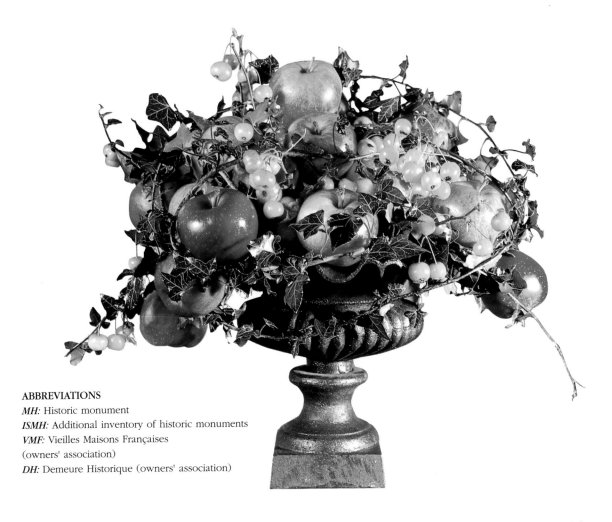

ABBREVIATIONS
MH: Historic monument
ISMH: Additional inventory of historic monuments
VMF: Vieilles Maisons Françaises
(owners' association)
DH: Demeure Historique (owners' association)

Alphabetical Index

*O*wning a château is source of never-ending joy and permanent
worry. To all those who welcomed us and showed such patience,
we should like to express again our grateful thanks.

GRAPHIC CONCEPTION
Brigitte Racine

© 1998 - Édilarge SA - Éditions Ouest-France, Rennes
Imprimé en janvier 1999 par l'Imprimerie Mame à Tours (37)
I.S.B.N. 2.7373.2355.X - Dépôt légal : février 1998
N° éditeur : 3743.02.03.01.99